A Florida Pioneer

The Henschens, Partial Family Tree

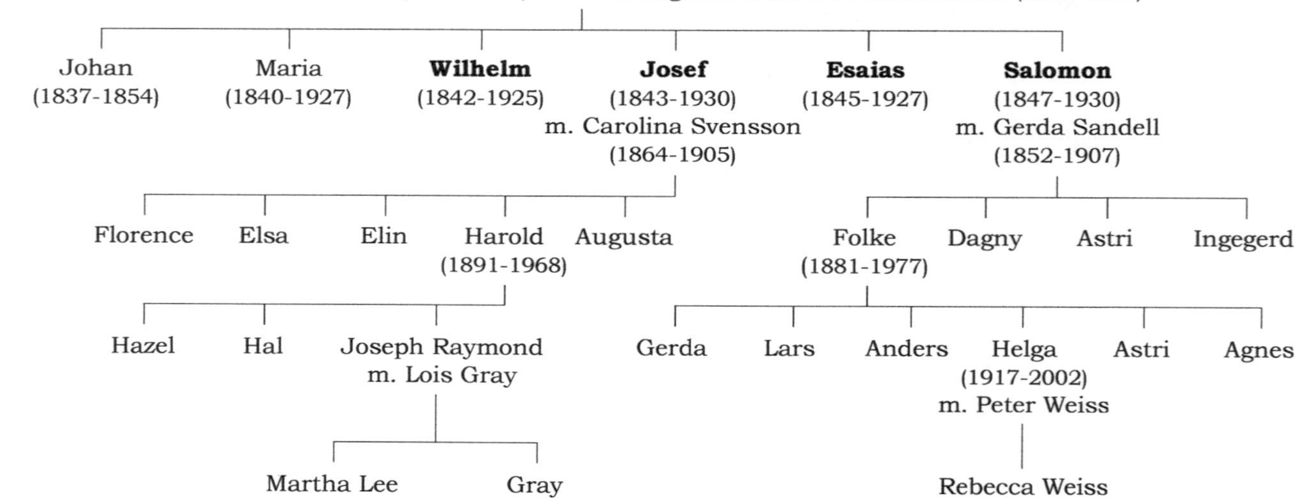

Many, many more people belong to this tree. This is just an illustration of the people mentioned in this book.
Sofia Sjöborg, L.W. Henschen's cousin, lived 1805-1883, and **Knut Ångström**, Josef Henschen's friend, lived 1857-1910.

A Florida Pioneer

The adventurous life of Josef Henschen, Swedish immigrant in the 1870s

*researched, translated,
edited and introduced
by Rebecca Weiss*

Book Design by DWC Publishing,
www.dwcpublishing.com

Cover: The Henschen homestead in the Lake Jesup
settlement, Florida, painted by Hasse Bergman in 1872.

ISBN-10: 1-84728-048-X
ISBN-13: 978-1-84728-048-0

Printed 2006 in the United States by Lulu Press

*To my dear cousin Veronica,
another of Josef's great-great
nieces, who followed the
development of this book.
To my mother Helga, who
would have loved to read it.
And to Christine Kinlaw-Best,
who helped so much with the
research.*

Contents

Acknowledgements

The first person to thank is Christine Kinlaw-Best, researcher at the Sanford Museum, who has published her own books about Seminole County history. Her information, interest and generosity, and the continuous dialogue with her have been of enormous help.

Joseph Raymond Henschen and his wife Lois took me on two journeys in Florida. I am very grateful for their help and kindness and for sharing their letters, photos and memories with me.

My cousin Laila Nygren in Sweden gave me a wonderful gift—the original painting of the Henschen homestead, which can be seen on the cover of this book.

Knut Ångström (the younger) sent me letters, photos and advice.

Robert Lugn and Kristina Lugn sent photos and information about their grandfather and great-grandfather Esaias Henschen.

Ellen Henschen in Atlanta, Georgia sent a family tree, and helped me locate Joseph Raymond in Florida.

Caroline Soka provided memories and a photo of her grandmother Carolina Henschen.

Alicia Clarke, curator of Sanford Museum, gave help and advice.

I want to thank Professor Gary Mormino at the University of South Florida, for his enthusiasm about my manuscript.

Thank you to Ellen Hersh, Jeri Johnson, Heinz Gewing, Herb Rizzardini, Elisabeth Auer, Madeleine Åhlstedt and Gun Lanciai, for reading the manuscript and giving important feedback.

Last but not least I am grateful to my husband Stu Sjouwerman for his patience, love and support, and for handling all my computer problems...

Introduction

"The Steamship Columbia on the Atlantic Ocean
October 16, 1871

My dear beloved Knut!
    You once said to me: 'Leave, without saying a word, just leave.' I remember it so well. It was last spring when I jokingly asked if I should go to America. Now I have followed your advice, against myself. Please don't be sad. You are so dear to me, and it would have been too painful to say goodbye before a trip like this one. I do not know when we will meet again. It is my intention to return next year, but all too often I have found that things don't work out as planned. If we will not meet again in this life, rest assured that in me you have had, and have, a *friend.*"

So began the first letter from my great-great uncle Josef Henschen, to his dear friend Knut Ångström in Sweden. Indeed, things often don't work out as planned, and Josef did not return to Sweden the next year. In fact, he stayed in America the rest of his life. From Florida, he kept writing to Knut.

When I was a child in Stockholm, my mother Helga used to tell me about Josef. He was her grandfather Salomon's brother, who in 1871 had left Upsala, Sweden, to settle in Orange County, Florida. I didn't know then where Florida was, but I understood it was a beautiful place, and that Josef was a remarkable man.

Salomon had two more brothers, Wilhelm and Esaias, who also went to America around the same time. Josef, Wilhelm and Esaias brought large groups of Swedes to work for Henry S. Sanford in east central Florida. Sanford and the Swedes founded the New Upsala settlement. Josef also helped to found St. Petersburg, Florida.

Of the three brothers, it was Josef who became a legend in the Henschen family. During his long life he wrote many letters to friends and family in Sweden. He told stories of living in the jungle, of fighting bears and alligators, of nearly dying of thirst and exposure, and of building orange groves and railroads. The Swedish relatives, who lived comfortable and protected lives, were in awe of Josef.

Three times Josef went back to visit the old country. The first time he brought along an alligator, which he let loose in a canal near Stockholm! Later the alligator, hungry and cold, was found on a field by a farmer. It was killed, stuffed and donated to Vänersborgs Museum in southwestern Sweden. There it is still on display, 130 years later, as the one and only alligator ever found in the wild in Sweden!

The second time Josef brought Spanish moss, which looked just like his own long gray beard. He also brought beautiful sea shells and strange objects that nobody in the Swedish family had ever seen. The Spanish moss was saved by Salomon's son Folke (my grandfather), and then by Folke's children, Helga and her siblings. They named it "Uncle Josef's beard."

Helga said Josef was a very special person, adventurous, enthusiastic and courageous. He was a respected and important member of the Swedish community of Orange County, and none of the Swedes would make any major decisions without consulting him.

Wilhelm, the oldest brother, eventually settled in Illinois. Esaias returned to Sweden after a few years in

America. Josef stayed in Florida, where he died in 1930 at age eighty-seven.

Through some twist of fate I, four generations later, ended up not far from the places where Wilhelm, Esaias and Josef arrived in 1871, and where Josef spent the rest of his life. Like my mother, grandfather and great-grandfather, I had been born and raised in Sweden. But I traveled widely, and in 1994 I moved to America, to a small town in Florida called Belleair.

I knew that Josef had been instrumental in founding my neighboring city, St. Petersburg, and that he might have descendants in Florida, but strangely enough I was never interested. That changed in the spring of 2005.

Having been a visual artist all my adult life, I made a slight change of direction in 2001, and started to write short stories. In 2004 I had finished and published my first book, an autobiography, and was looking for a new writing project. One day I got a letter from a lady named Lynn Faulkner, who lives in New Mexico. I had never met her and did not know of her existence, but she said she was a distant relative. She had done a search on the name Henschen on the Internet, and found me through my mother's web site, www.HelgaHenschen.com. Lynn and I began a correspondence. She thought she was related to Josef Henschen, but wasn't sure how. I became curious and started to do some research. Eventually I located Josef's grandson, Joseph Raymond Henschen, who was around eighty years old, in St. Cloud, Florida.

In May 2005 I visited Joseph Raymond and his wife Lois. Joseph R. was a retired dentist who had been working in his profession until only a few years ago. He had recently taken up the guitar, and played beautifully. He also made exquisite jewelry, having acquired his skills with silver and gold as a dentist. Lois had become a quilt-maker when she retired, and their house was full of gorgeous quilts she had made.

Joseph R. and Lois were healthy and young at heart, just like Joseph R.'s grandfather Josef, and like *my* grandfather Folke and mother Helga had been. Joseph R. and Lois were very hospitable, and happy to talk about their ancestors. They took me to the small town of Oakland, where Josef had lived, and showed me where his house had been. It was near Lake Apopka, which Josef had described in his letters. Around the corner was Henschen Avenue, named after Josef. We saw the Town Hall which had once been the post office where Josef served as postmaster, and we went to the cemetery to see his grave. It was clean and well kept, with large oaks and palm trees around it.

We also visited the orange groves Josef had started in the 1870s. When he grew too old to care for them, he turned them over to his children. His son Harald became the manager. Harald later gave the orchards to his children, with his son Joseph R. as manager. A few years ago the orchards had been sold, and were no longer in any Henschen possession. I stole an orange anyway, and found it delicious. It was strange to consider what these orchards had meant to three generations of Henschens, and the hardships Josef went through when all the orange trees froze and died in the mid-1890s.

Half a year later I took another trip with Joseph R. and Lois. This time we went to the Sanford Museum, where we met Alicia Clarke, the curator, and Christine Kinlaw-Best, an extremely knowledgeable and energetic historical researcher. We studied many documents. Christine and I had already been corresponding for months before we finally met in person. Together we visited the part of Sanford where New Upsala used to be. There was still an Upsala Road, an Upsala Swedish cemetery, and a beautiful little Presbyterian church built by the Swedes in the 1890s.

Joseph Raymond Henschen, grandson of Josef, by the Henschen orange groves in May 2005.

Henschen Avenue in Oakland, Florida.

Josef and Carolina Henschen's headstone in the Oakland cemetery.

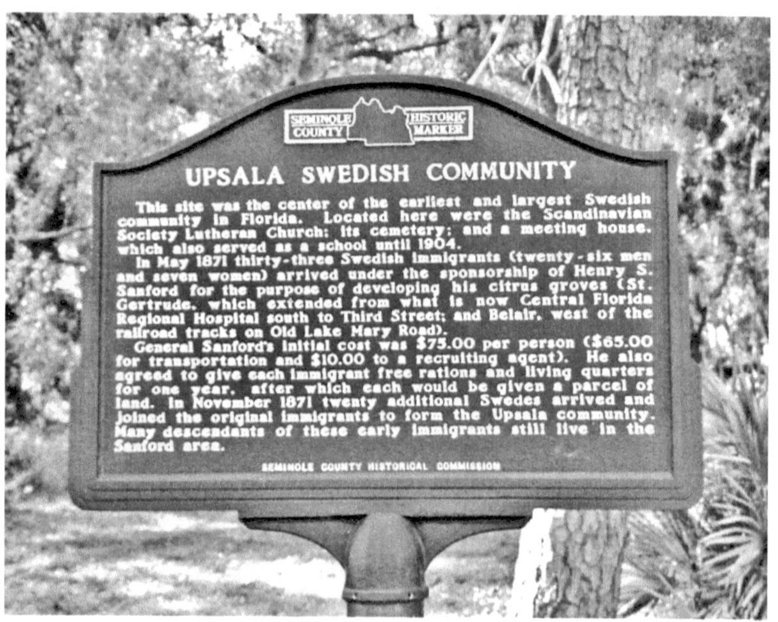

Plaque by Upsala Cemetery, Sanford. The text begins with: "This site was the center of the earliest and largest Swedish community in Florida."

Upsala Presbyterian Church, built 1892, still beautiful in 2006.

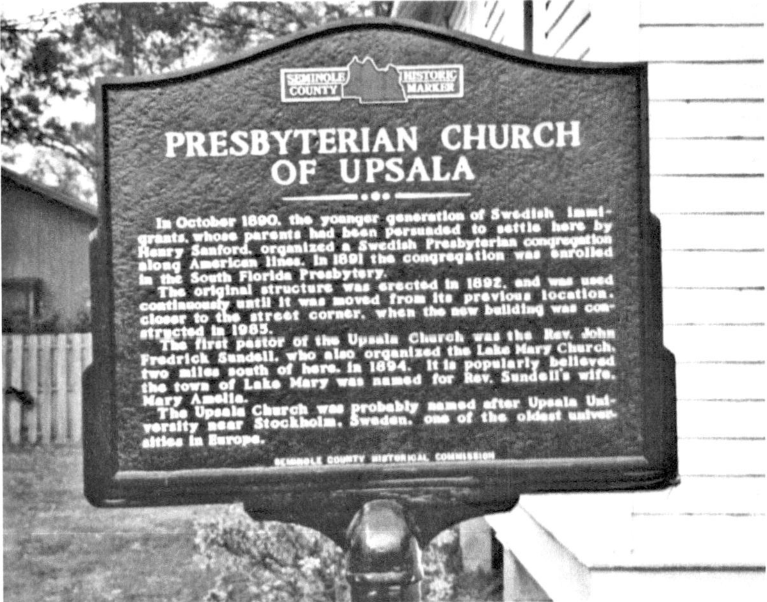

Plaque by the church.

Upsala Road in Sanford.

In May, Joseph R. had given me twenty letters in Swedish, written by his grandfather between 1871 and 1923. Most of them were addressed to Josef's friend Knut Ångström in Sweden. They had been transcribed from the original handwritten ones. Each letter was several pages, and it took me a few hours to get through them. They were moving and amazing, and I sometimes cried when I read them. After getting permission to use the letters, both from Joseph R. and from Knut's grandson in Sweden, I decided to try to publish something about Josef and his family.

I have done my own translation of Josef's letters, and edited them in some places to make them easier for modern readers to understand. Some repetitious parts, or descriptions that were too complicated and confusing, have been left out. However, anything that could possibly have historical importance has stayed in. The transcriber of the letters to Knut said that Josef's handwriting was hard to decipher, and that there might be errors in the transcripts. When I felt there were errors I tried to correct them, usually with the help of Christine Best.

Later I acquired photocopies of a number of handwritten letters from Josef to his father Lars, and to his brother, my great-grandfather Salomon (in Swedish), dating up to 1930. These came from the Henschen Archives at the Uppsala University Library in Sweden and had not been transcribed. They were often illegible, so I understand what the transcriber of the letters to Knut meant. I also got a few of Esaias' letters, which were equally hard to decipher.

I might mention that I have definite disagreements with some of Josef's opinions and activities. Like all of us, Josef had his good and bad sides. I do feel that his good sides by far outweigh the bad, and that he was quite a captivating personality.

In 1874, Josef's brother Wilhelm wrote an instruction book for Swedes who were considering immigration to Florida. I translated that one as well. It can now be found in the Sanford Museum, and is a good complement to Josef's letters.

The Henschen family in Upsala, Sweden in the late 1860s. Front row from left to right: Maria, Lars, Sofia Sjöborg (Lars' cousin), Wilhelm. Behind them, from left to right: Salomon, Esaias, Josef (standing), Hanna (Wilhelm's wife).

The Upsala Family

This story begins in the early 1800s, in the town of Upsala, about 75 kilometers north of Stockholm, Sweden. (Later the spelling was changed to Uppsala.) It is a quaint old town, dating back to the 13th century. Its famous university, founded in 1477, is the oldest in Scandinavia.

Lars Wilhelm Henschen was born in 1805, in the county of Blekinge in southern Sweden, but lived in Upsala most of his life. He could trace his family tree back to 1620, when a young man named Andreas Henschen arrived in Sweden from Brandenburg, Germany. From his early youth, Lars was interested in political and social issues, in the temperance movement, and in religious questions. He was a county judge, and a great advocate of religious freedom, which was courageous in those days when religious minorities were heavily persecuted. His motto was "Freedom and Love". One of the people he helped and defended was Erik Jansson, founder of the Jansonite pietistic society, who was jailed for his beliefs. In 1850, when Jews still did not have full civil rights, Lars gained permission for a Jewish man, Albert Bonnier, to open a bookstore in Upsala. In 1853 Lars became a member of the Swedish Parliament.

He married Augusta Munck af Rosenschöld, one year his junior. She was a noblewoman from an illustrious family. Like Lars, her father was a county judge. Her brother Eberhard was a medical doctor who emigrated to Paraguay. There he became the personal physician of the cruel and merciless dictator, Solano Lopez, who eventually had Eberhard tortured and killed.

Augusta and Lars had five sons and one daughter, all born and raised in Upsala. Their oldest son Johan was born in 1837. Then Maria came in 1840. She was a gifted child who later founded the Henschen School for Girls. Maria—called Mia—did things women didn't normally do in the 1800s. She rode horses without a saddle, swam long distances, and dived in deep waters. She learned six foreign languages. If she had been a man, or lived fifty years later, she could have become something great, but there were few opportunities then for women. She married, divorced, and married again, which was also unheard-of. Like her father and brothers she was deeply religious. She wrote books about spiritualism and occultism and always spoke her mind, no matter how unpopular. Both my mother and grandfather, in their memoirs, describe Maria as a formidable woman.

She lived her last years in a nursing home, but even when she was close to ninety, her mind was crystal-clear.

This is what her nurse reported about her death:

"It was 11:00 p.m. Mrs. Maria von Bergen said to me: At midnight, I want you to leave the room, because that is when God is coming."

Exactly at midnight Maria died.

Wilhelm, the second son, was born in 1842. Josef was born in 1843, Esaias in 1845, and my great-grandfather Salomon in 1847.

Augusta, their mother, did not have an easy life. Her husband Lars spent most of his time in the Stockholm Parliament, and she seldom saw him. In the 1850s, when her children were still young, Augusta contracted tuberculosis. She died in 1856, only fifty years old. Her heart had been broken by the death of her oldest son, Johan, two years earlier when he was seventeen. My grandfather Folke said Johan probably also had tuberculosis.

An unmarried cousin of Lars, Sofia Sjöborg, moved in with the family when Augusta fell ill. Sofia was a tiny woman, and far from pretty, as can be seen in the family photo from the late 1860s. She was a good and generous person. Wilhelm later wrote: "I had the inestimable blessing of growing up under the personal guidance of a motherly friend, a first cousin of my father, Sofia Sjöborg. She lived in our home as a member of the family, and when my mother was incapacitated by sickness, she became a second mother to me. Her words and prayers, and above all her sainted and unselfish life, are to me an inheritance worth more than any riches."

When Wilhelm, as the first of the Henschen brothers, emigrated to America in 1871, he asked Sofia to come with him. It was brave of Sofia to start a new life on a new continent, at age sixty-six. Although excited about the emigration, she was sad to leave the rest of the Henschen family in Sweden, knowing she would never see some of them again.

In her own diary from that time, she displayed her optimistic spirit. There was not a word of complaint about the long and strenuous journey. Instead she praised God. "I feel so happy at sea, nothing disturbs my peace. Resting in God's bosom, I am secure in Jesus" she wrote. "I thank God I have been able to live a *life* and not lain dormant or in lethargy."

Sofia must have had quite an influence not only on Wilhelm but on all the children—encouraging spiritual awareness, fearlessness and gratitude for any blessings bestowed on them. The only sibling who did not share her piety was Salomon, the youngest, my great-grandfather. Salomon was not religious, and refused confirmation in the State Church. However, my mother Helga loved him and described him as a kind and affectionate grandfather. Salomon, in his own autobiography, says:

"In spite of all the difficulties, I have had a magnificent life, which I would like to live all over again."

Lars Henschen encouraged his children to travel and see the world. Maria made journeys to many European countries. Salomon spent two years in Brazil 1867-69, exploring the jungle, but returned home to establish himself as a doctor. The other three brothers went to America.

Before going to the U.S., Wilhelm and Esaias had studied at the philosophy department of Upsala University. Josef and Salomon trained in the medical faculty.

Salomon was passionate about his work. He became a well known doctor and professor of medicine, one of the foremost in Europe. When Lenin, the founder of the Soviet Union, lay dying in St. Petersburg / Leningrad in 1923, the best specialists from all over Europe were called to his sickbed in an attempt to save his life. Salomon was one of the doctors summoned, and Folke, who was also a doctor, was allowed to come along with his father. This journey became another family legend—Salomon and Folke by Lenin's bedside. Many stories about this event were told to me and my cousins. One of the souvenirs Salomon was given in Russia was a kind of helmet, worn by the red army soldiers. I have inherited this helmet, and always feel a certain awe when I look at it.

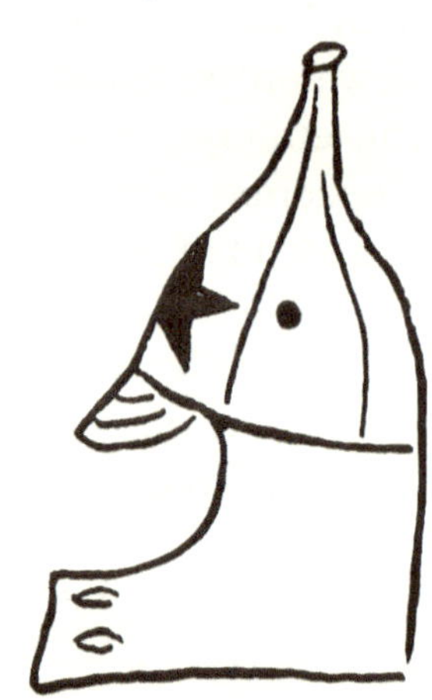

*Red army helmet
from 1923.*

(There are several family connections to St. Petersburg, Russia. Josef gave this name to the city in Florida in 1887, and I myself made a most memorable and frightening trip to the Russian city in 1984, when it was still in the Soviet Union and called Leningrad.)

Salomon Henschen on his 80th birthday, February 28, 1927.

Folke Henschen, forty years old, 1921.

The Henschen men were tall and skinny, with light brown hair and blue eyes, and were generally healthy and energetic. Quite a few of them were in the medical profession. My grandfather Folke became a professor of medicine at Karolinska Institutet in Stockholm, just like his father Salomon. For decades, Folke was a member of the Medical Nobel Committee, and was its chairman 1942-46. (This is the committee that decides who will get the Nobel Prize in medicine each year.) Folke remembered the very first Nobel Prize Ceremony in 1901, which he attended as a twenty-year-old medical student. He liked to tell funny stories from that event.

I visited Folke a few weeks before his death, when he was ninety-six years old. He was still mentally clear, and working on a new scientific thesis. He used to frequently tell us grandchildren that it was healthy to be thin, and that we should all keep our weight down if we wanted to live long lives. This worked for him, for his siblings, and for his children, who all lived well into their eighties or nineties.

Swedish Emigration

In Sweden in the mid- and late 1800s, emigration to America was one of the big questions. The population of the country was growing rapidly and had actually doubled between 1750 and 1850. There were not many cities in Sweden, not much industry, and many people tried to live from agriculture. But there was not enough good farmland. Most people were very poor, not able to own land or to survive on the land they owned. 1867, 68, and 69 were particularly bad years for Swedish agriculture. Those who lived in the cities also had a hard time making a living. Nearly 60,000 Swedes emigrated during those years.

Then there was religious persecution. All Swedes were automatically members of the State Lutheran Church, from birth. This was still the case until 1996! You had to *apply* to leave the state church! Until 1858 you were fined, jailed or exiled for practicing other Christian faiths! Even later, when these penalties were abolished, there was religious intolerance and persecution. This is another reason many Swedes left. Full religious freedom was not granted by law until 1951!

In the mid-1800s there was a religious awakening all over Europe, including Sweden. People yearned for religious freedom. One of the first non-state churches started in Sweden was the Baptist congregation, founded there in 1848. This was illegal, and the founder was exiled. In 1858, six Swedish women who had converted to Catholicism were exiled. Other non-state Christian groups fared just as badly.

(Strangely enough, it seems that the Jews in Sweden were subjected to less persecution than the Christian minorities. For the Jews, who had suffered terribly in Russia and many European countries, Sweden became a relatively safe haven. The first Jew arrived in Sweden in 1774, by special permission from the king. He was allowed to bring some friends and relatives and to start a congregation the next year. However, the Jews could only live in certain cities, and practice a limited number of trades. They were not allowed to marry Christians. In 1870 they finally received full civil rights.

After that they quickly became highly assimilated. When my grandfather Folke in 1909 married Signe Thiel, my grandmother, who came from one of the oldest Swedish-Jewish families, their cultural differences were hardly noticeable.)

Military conscription was another unpopular institution in Sweden. Some young men left for that reason alone.

Like in other European countries, the class system was very rigid. It was practically impossible to advance in society if you were born to the "wrong" parents or economic background.

By contrast with many poor people in other parts of Europe, the Swedes were literate. In the mid-1800s almost all children, regardless of social status, were sent to school, where they at least learned to read and write. This was usually not sufficient to get a good job and make a decent living, but it did enable them to read about America in newspapers and advertising, and to plan their emigration.

Then there were those who emigrated "just for fun" like the Henschen brothers. They belonged to the privileged class and could easily have made good careers in Sweden. But they were romantic adventurers who dreamed of a more exciting life. They certainly got what they wanted, especially Josef.

Wilhelm, Esaias and Sofia

Like many of the Henschens, Wilhelm was a multi-talented person. By the late 1860s he had a Ph. D. and a teaching job at the Upsala University. During his long life he would also be a businessman, farmer, writer, newspaper editor, and a Methodist preacher. In 1868 he married Hanna Lilljebjörn, (1844-1922) who bore their first child in 1870.

Wilhelm was the first of the Henschen brothers to go to America. His earliest visit, accompanied by his young brother-in-law Henrik Lilljebjörn, was in September 1870. Wilhelm bought some land in the small settlement of Lake Jesup, Florida. I don't know for sure why Wilhelm picked this spot, but speculate that he may have been inspired by the famous Swedish author Fredrika Bremer (1801-1865). Bremer traveled down the St. Johns River to Lake Monroe (very close to Lake Jesup), as early as 1850, and wrote about it in her book *Homes of the New World*. She described the area as unbelievably beautiful. My guess is that Fredrika Bremer and Lars Henschen knew each other—they were of the same generation, had many interests in common and must have belonged to the same social circles.

Although Wilhelm owned land in Florida, he spent most of his time in New York. There he did business with Anchor Lines shipping company, and its agents the Henderson Brothers. He changed his first name to William. He persuaded Swedes to come to the U.S., sold tickets for Anchor, and made deals with U.S. plantation owners.

A ticket Wilhelm provided for a Swedish immigrant. Wilhelm's signature is at the bottom. (Courtesy of the Sanford Museum.)

The most important of these planters was Henry Shelton Sanford (1823-1891). He was an attorney and for some years a U.S. Minister to Belgium. The town Sanford in east central Florida is named after him. In May 1870, Henry Sanford bought more than 12,000 acres of land in Seminole County, Florida, by the St. Johns River. (At that time it was still called Orange County.) Mr. Sanford started two large orange groves, and hired local blacks (mostly newly freed slaves) and whites to work in them. For some reason, none of them were to his satisfaction. Also there were problems between the whites and blacks—jealous white workers shot and wounded several black ones. Sanford began to look for other, different workers. Wilhelm Henschen, then in New York, heard that Sanford needed laborers. He contacted Sanford and offered to bring in Swedish workers for the plantations. Swedes were known to be hard-working, honest and able.

Wilhelm already had experience in finding Swedish workers for planters in Florida and other states. The agreement was usually that the American employer would pay the passage and travel expenses for the Swedes, who in exchange would work at his plantations for one year. They would get food and lodging, but no wages during that year. After one year they would start getting wages, and could begin negotiations to get their families in Sweden sent over. Henry Sanford also offered to give each Swedish family 5 acres of land for their own use, after one year of labor.

Sanford and Wilhelm began a correspondence. The first letter from Wilhelm dates February 15, 1871, and can be found in the Sanford Museum. The two men made a deal where Wilhelm would go to Sweden, recruit workers and bring them over to Sanford. Wilhelm would get paid $8.50 per worker, and all expenses covered. He also bargained to get some of his own family members over for free.

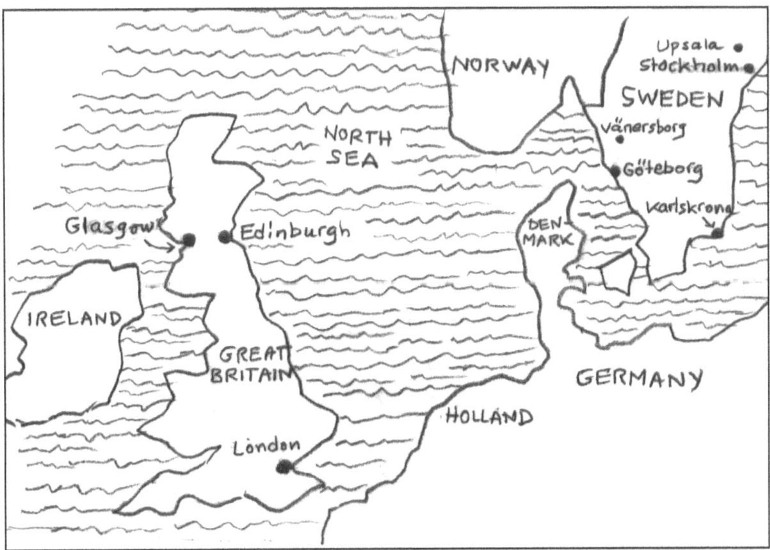

Map of northern Europe.

Wilhelm went back to Sweden, and returned in April 1871 with his brother Esaias, his aunt Sofia Sjöborg, and about fifty Swedish workers he had recruited. Thirty-two of these would go to Sanford in Florida. Wilhelm's wife Hanna and infant daughter remained in Sweden for the time being, arriving a few months later together with his brother Josef.

Sofia vividly described this journey in her diary. On April 18, 1871, the Swedish group left Upsala by train, for Göteborg (Gothenburg) in southwestern Sweden. Some of the other immigrants Sofia mentioned were Thieman, Ernlund, Andersson, Löfgren, Wass, Lindberg, Johansson, Wennström, Robert Almgren, and a girl named Julia Lundquist.

From Göteborg they sailed with the *SS Scandinavia* to Edinburgh on the east coast of Great Britain. A train took them across Scotland to Glasgow on the west coast, where they joined groups of Scottish, Irish and German passengers. They boarded the *SS Anglia*, which departed on April 29 for New York City.

On May 11, 1871, at dusk, they reached New York. Here they entered Castle Garden, a huge building which had once been a theatre that could hold several thousand spectators. Officials recorded their names, ages and professions. Germans, Scots, Irish and Swedes were then shown to separate quarters. In this building they were safe, and if they wanted, they could stay a couple of days. There was food for sale, although quite expensive. After eating bread, cheese and milk, most of the immigrants fell asleep on the mattresses they had brought with them. There was tremendous noise in the building. People were talking, laughing and playing music everywhere, but the Swedes had become used to such noise on the ship, and were able to sleep through it.

Only immigrants were allowed inside Castle Garden, but outside the building a host of swindlers and gangsters, known as "runners" were waiting. When the immigrants ventured outside, they were harassed by these runners, who tried to convince them to go to work for other plantation owners than the ones who had paid their trips. The runners also tried to sell them useless merchandise or give them all kinds of fraudulent help and advice. Wilhelm had warned the Swedes about the runners.

Some of the Swedes from the *SS Anglia* went by train to various parts of America, like Minnesota, Wisconsin, or the town of New Sweden in Maine. Some went with Wilhelm by boat to the Sanford plantation in Florida. Sofia, Wilhelm, Esaias and about thirty other Swedes boarded the *SS Dictator*, bound for Charleston, South Carolina. The crew consisted mainly of black men, and a number of the passengers were also black. Most of the Swedes had never seen black people before they came to America. When the Swedes sat on deck singing religious hymns, some black passengers joined in, humming the tune.

They disembarked in Charleston which had a very lively harbor. Mules pulled wagons laden with merchandise, and bales of cotton were unloaded and loaded onto the multitude of ships. The Swedes took a walk in the colorful town. Sofia was impressed by the large, beautiful homes, the shady verandas and gardens full of flowers.

The next leg of the journey was on another boat, bound for Savannah, Georgia. They slept in spacious cabins on third deck, and were given delicious Florida orange juice which they had never tasted before. In the evening they stopped in Jacksonville, Florida. From there they went down the St. Johns River on a small propeller steamboat. It was a pleasant and quiet trip. The banks were covered with dense growth and forest, and gray moss was hanging from the trees. They were told this moss was used to stuff mattresses. Sofia spotted gray eagles, wild ducks, and alligators swimming along the banks. In several places there were clearings for new settlements. At one point a thunderstorm swept over them, and lightning illuminated the water. Some passengers were frightened, and started praying fervently, but Sofia was intrigued by the beauty of nature and the grace of God.

The St. Johns River runs into Lake Monroe in east central Florida. On May 30, 1871, they arrived in Mellonville on the southern shore of the lake. This was a small village consisting of a few houses, a store and some sheds. (Today, Mellonville is part of Sanford.) The workers thanked Wilhelm for his management of the journey, and were then taken to one of Henry Sanford's plantations. Wilhelm, Esaias and Sofia had to stay in Mellonville for three days, in one of the sheds. They didn't have much food left, and there was nothing to buy except coffee and cookies. One day they found turtles, which they caught and made soup of.

On the third evening they went on board again and traveled all night down the St. Johns River which ran into another large lake, Lake Jesup. (Later the spelling was changed to Jessup.) In the morning they arrived at Solary's wharf on its southern side. There they found a store where they could buy baked goods and blueberries. A Mr. Duval ("a gentleman of excellent upbringing") arrived with a long wagon and mules, and they were taken to Mr. Lawton's farm which was situated by a small lake with hammock forest around it. Its name was simply Round Lake. There their luggage was unloaded.

Next day they went to Wilhelm's property which was on the other side of Round Lake. A tent was set up, as there was no house on the lot. Yet Sofia did not complain. The June temperatures did not bother her—cool showers fell, and a fresh wind was blowing. Everyone was in good health. Wilhelm dug a little canal around the tent so that the rain water could run off. From Mr. Lawton he purchased a sow with six piglets, and some young orange trees. They began to build a

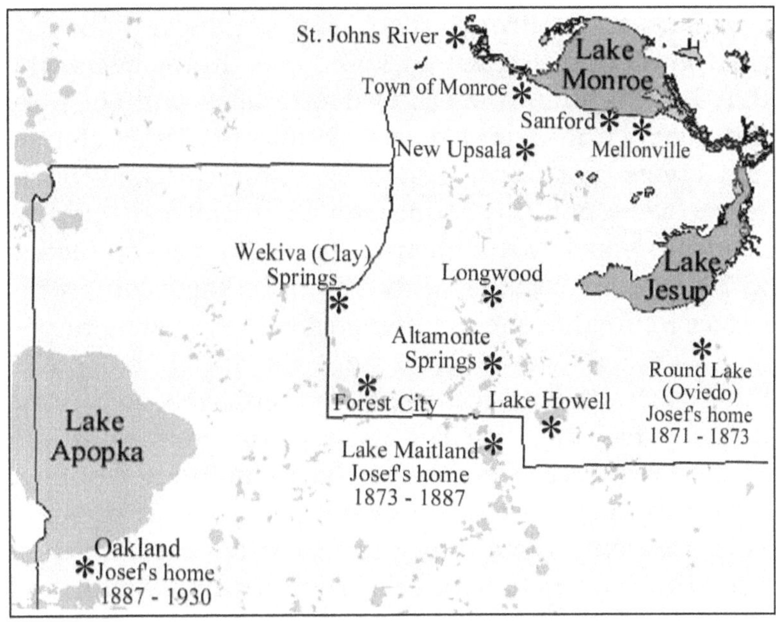

Orange and Seminole counties. To the lower left is Lake Apopka and Oakland where Josef Henschen lived the later part of his life. To the right are Lake Monroe and Mellonville, where the Swedes arrived in 1871. Below Lake Jesup is the tiny Round Lake where Wilhelm Henschen bought his first piece of land. (Courtesy of Christine Best.)

house. Gradually they got to know their neighbors, the Lawtons, the Duvals, and a Miss Putnam.

The community was known as the Lake Jesup colony, although it was not directly on that lake. Lake Jesup was the nearest *large* lake, much larger than Round Lake. Within a few years the Jesup colony would be absorbed into Oviedo, its adjacent town.

The Swedish laborers started working at the Sanford plantations. Soon they found that the conditions were very hard. They had to work ten to twelve hours a day, from five in the morning until sundown, (with a two-and-a-half-hour siesta) five days a week, and five or six hours on Saturdays. Their food consisted of beans, rice, potatoes and some pork and beef. In the beginning they had to stay in overcrowded houses and sleep on the floor without mattresses or sheets. Their clothes and shoes wore out, and they didn't get new ones. These were not the conditions they had expected or been promised. Wilhelm tried to rectify the problems, with some success. By July 1872, Esaias wrote in his letters home that most of Sanford's Swedes were happy and satisfied. However, some were not. Some broke their contracts and were severely penalized. According to historian Christine Best, few of the Swedes stayed long enough with Sanford to claim the 5 acres of land they were supposed to receive after one year of labor. There are only records of eight Swedes receiving their free land. The rest, who had tried to run away or had stirred up trouble among the others, did not receive it. But many Swedes stayed in the area anyway, buying their own land.

In the summer of 1871, Mr. Sanford asked Wilhelm to return to Sweden and recruit more Swedes to come and work for him. He wanted men with specific trades and professions, and a few women to work as cooks.

Wilhelm agreed, but fell ill in New York and couldn't travel to Sweden. He then cabled his brother Josef to come instead, and bring thirty-six Swedish workers with him. Josef hesitated, but finally decided to do it. While he was selecting the workers, he wrote to Mr. Sanford (in German, strangely enough) about the difficulties he was having. Carpenters and masons were especially hard to recruit. They were paid $1.11 per day in Sweden, and they felt, not without reason, that one year was too long a time to work in exchange for their travel expenses. But in the end Josef got his workers and took them to Florida.

In 1874, Wilhelm wrote the book called *Sanford*. It was intended to encourage more Swedes to come to America, and to central Florida especially. He appealed to the poor and oppressed farmers and workers, tempting them with freedom and prosperity. He described in detail how they could benefit from working with Mr. Sanford. They would have a good chance of becoming rich landowners and securing a good future for their children. He praised Florida, saying it had the best climate and best soil in the U.S. For some crops the soil was the best in the whole world! The winters were wonderful, and the summers cool and pleasant, never too hot...

(This may be surprising information for current Florida residents. Anybody who lives here knows that Florida summers are unbearably hot and humid! The climate has apparently changed. In the 1870s most of the state was still covered by dense forest and high trees. The population was sparse, and there wasn't much industry. All these factors may have made the summers cooler than they are now.)

Anyone who had a cheerful disposition, was strong, healthy and persistent, and willing to work hard, should immigrate to America, Wilhelm said. "Help yourself and God will help you." He advised the Swedes on which possessions to bring to the States, and which to leave at home. He told them to beware of theft on the boat, and to be polite and tolerant during the journey...

Until the mid-1870s Wilhelm divided his time between New York and Florida, spending more and more time in New York. There, he was for some time the secretary of the famous inventor John Ericsson. Wilhelm was also the editor of *Norden*, a Swedish language weekly newspaper that relayed news about both Sweden and America to Swedish immigrants.

In 1875 Wilhelm became a Methodist preacher and moved to Chicago. There he worked as an instructor in the Swedish Methodist Theological Seminary, and as an editor of *Sändebudet,* the organ of the Swedish Methodist churches in America. He did this until his retirement in 1911. Wilhelm and his wife Hanna had seven children and many grandchildren.

Esaias was an even more devoted Christian than Wilhelm and Josef. In his letters from Florida in the early 1870s to his father in Sweden, he constantly described his longing for God and divine peace. He considered becoming a priest or perhaps even a monk. However, in 1875 he married a Swedish girl named Emelia Magnusson. For some time they lived in St. Augustine, where Esaias was a Justice of the Peace. In 1879 they returned to Sweden, where they had two daughters, two grandsons and several great-grandchildren. Esaias became the director of a bank in Upsala, and died at age eighty-two.

Josef and Knut

Josef as a young man.   Knut as a young man.

(Courtesy of Knut Ångström.)

Now we come to Josef, the main "hero" of this book.

In 1856, when Josef was only twelve years old, he started to help his father Lars with certain jobs in Upsala. Lars had been elected Member of Parliament and spent at least five days a week in Stockholm. He owned many buildings, with 306 rental units, but had no time to take care of the properties. Josef became the deputy landlord, collecting rent, writing receipts, and supervising the carpenters and painters who were constantly repairing the old wooden houses. Thus Josef, at a young age, became accustomed to business transactions and to handling workers and renters. He also liked boats, and went sailing whenever he could. These skills, both in handling laborers and in sailing, would prove useful later when he emigrated to Florida.

When Josef's mother died in 1854, and his sister Maria was sent to a high-class boarding school, all social life in their home stopped. Subsequently, Josef didn't have much female company. He became very shy with girls—a shyness that lasted all his life. He was more comfortable with other boys and with children.

In the 1860s Josef studied medicine, zoology and botany at the Upsala University.

One day when he was working in his laboratory, a six-year-old child suddenly wandered in. Josef was surprised and amused, and they started a conversation. This child was Knut Ångström, son of the famous Swedish scientist Anders Jonas Ångström. (The unit "angstrom" which some of us may remember from our Physics classes in school, is named after him. An angstrom is one hundred-millionth of a centimeter, and is used to express the wavelength of light and other radiations.)

Something happened deep in Josef's soul when he met this child. A chord was struck. Josef never forgot this first encounter with Knut, and described it in several letters, even as late as 1923, when Knut was long dead and Josef was an old man. Knut became Josef's friend forever, no matter what happened, no matter how many decades passed, no matter what disagreements they had.

Their personalities were very different. Knut, although charming and gifted, was introverted, prone to illness, and often depressed. Josef was outgoing, cheerful and optimistic, and fourteen years older than Knut. Apart from their scientific interests they did not have much in common, yet they developed a profound affection for each other. With the exception of his own children, Josef loved Knut more than any other person in his life—more than his own wife or his parents or siblings.

Josef's letters to Knut were discovered more than hundred years later, by Knut's grandson, whose name is also Knut Ångström. He found them in his father's attic. Eventually Knut had them transcribed, and sent copies to Joseph Raymond in Florida.

Knut's letters to Josef were lost in a fire. But Josef's letters, written over several decades, paint a fascinating picture both of his love for Knut, of his own life, and of Florida history.

Some people have speculated over Josef's feelings for Knut. Was Josef in love with the boy? Was there a physical relationship? Some of Josef's letters may make it seem that way. Personally, I doubt that this was ever the case. I think people in the 1800s were much more affectionate and romantic in the way they addressed each other, than they are today. I have seen letters written to my grandparents and great-grandparents by friends and family members. They were also effusive and loving in a flowery style that people seldom use now. My opinion is that Josef's and Knut's relationship was intense, but platonic. Both of them later got married and fathered several children.

Josef left Sweden on October 10, 1871, on a ship bound for Scotland. With Josef were his sister-in-law Hanna and her baby, and their artist friend Hasse Bergman, as well as the workers Josef had recruited. In Scotland they embarked on the *SS Columbia* to New York City. Here is Josef's first letter to Knut.

Letter 1 from Josef to Knut

The Steamship Columbia on the Atlantic Ocean
October 16, 1871

My dear beloved Knut!
  You once said to me: "Leave, without saying a word, just leave." I remember it so well. It was last spring when I jokingly asked if I should go to America. Now I have followed your advice, against myself. Please don't be sad. You are so dear to me, and it would have been too painful to say goodbye before a trip like this one. I do not know when we will meet again. It is my intention to return next year, but all too often I have found that things don't work out as planned. If we will not meet again in this life, rest assured that in me you have had, and have, a *friend*.
  I so well recall my first encounter with you and the impression you made on me then. There are so many memories of times we spent together, that I cannot avoid thinking of you, when I recall the last eight years. Thank you a thousand times for this! I hope to see you soon again.
  Many circumstances worked together to make this journey a reality. The main one was that my brother Wilhelm, who was supposed to come home this autumn to pick up his wife Hanna, fell ill in New York. We did not want Hanna to travel alone. Wilhelm had also promised to find a number of Swedish workers and take them to Florida, but now he couldn't travel. He asked me to go in his place. First I declined, and found another man to accompany the workers. But then I had some disappointing experiences at the university, and decided to go after all. So now I am out on the great sea, far from family and friends. Forgive me, my dear boy, for not saying goodbye to you. Give my regards to your father, mother, sister and future brother-in-law. If you write to me, I will always answer. Perhaps I will be able

to entertain you with stories from another continent. It will be enjoyable and interesting to get out in the world, but it would have been better if I had more money. 200 Swedish kronor is all I have. Wilhelm paid my ticket, and currently I am doing all right. Cabin passage is quite comfortable. They spoil you with good food and service.

Later. This you should experience, Knut! We are having a terrible storm. The wind is howling in the riggings. The waves are getting higher and higher. This enormous ship is 22 feet below the water and two stories above it. It is leaning heavily to the side. If you stand in the stem or stern, you are thrown upward so that your knees bend uncontrollably, and then you plunge down into the deep so that you get dizzy. All while the masts squeak and creak. Now they are finally taking down the sails. We are about three hundred people onboard and most of them are seasick. I am not seasick, and I am very cheerful. I walk around, trying to cheer up others who are sick or frightened. This evening I visited a poor Irish family. I sang a happy Swedish song for them and gave them some camphor drops for the nausea. They immediately felt better.

When the weather is good we dance and sing.
(Rest of letter missing)

(My own comments, as well as excerpts from letters to other people than Knut and Knut's future wife, will be in italics.)

On November 2, 1871, the Columbia *arrived in New York. The Swedish group was met at the wharf by a brother-in-law of Henry Sanford, Charles DuPuy, who took them to Florida on another steamship. They arrived in Mellonville on November 7. In the group were twenty Swedish workers and two Englishmen, apart from Josef, Hasse, Hanna and her baby.*

Josef delivered the workers at Sanford's plantation, and then went to see his brothers and aunt Sofia at their Lake Jesup settlement. By this time they had built a house and were no longer living in a tent. Hasse Bergman made a watercolor painting of the Henschens' homestead. It pictures Wilhelm, Hanna, Esaias, Josef and Sofia, as well as a mule, a cow, pigs and chickens.

(Later, the house burned down. In 2006, Christine Best, with the help of land records and a photo of Bergman's painting, was able to pinpoint where the house had been—on the eastern shore of Round Lake, in today's Oviedo.)

Josef worked with his brothers for a few weeks, cutting wood and clearing land. In January 1872, he and Hasse decided to make a trip down the coast to get to know Florida.

(Following page)
The Henschen homestead on the eastern shore of Round Lake, painted by Hasse Bergman in 1871 or 1872. Most likely, it is Wilhelm working by the table, Sofia sitting in the back of the house, Josef cutting wood, Hanna standing in the door, baby Signe playing in front of the house, and Esaias riding on the mule. The couple to the left are probably neighbors. On the other side of the lake you see the Lawtons' home. The blue and yellow Swedish flag has one reddish corner—this is probably a small American flag. Notice the chickens and pigs. The original painting is only 6x11 inches, and these tiny shapes are painted in amazing detail.

Letter 2 from Josef to Knut

Everglades, January 1872

I am writing to you lying on a bear skin in an Indian *Wigissane*, where I, Hasse Bergman and an American acquaintance have spent the night. I am doing well, except that a dog bit me in the thigh last night, and except for the mosquitoes.

An old Indian Chief, Aleek, is sitting next to me. He is about a hundred years old and is contentedly smoking a pipe I gave him as a gift. Our *toutka* (fire) is burning, and coffee is being boiled in a pot. In the ashes we are frying yams that the Indians gave us. I have purchased a large amount of *ittjo* (dried deer meat). I brought tobacco, knives, angle hooks and other small items, and in exchange I got four tanned deer skins. They are making moccasins for me right now.

To start from the beginning; we walked, rowed and paddled 250 miles, along the ocean, down to the southern end of the Everglades. These cover about 200 miles, up to the middle of Florida. We went to the south because there we were more likely to meet Indians than in the northern part.

We often slept on the wet sand by the ocean, with the waves of the Atlantic roaring by our feet. It has been a rough journey, walking in the burning sun, carrying 50 pounds of weight on our shoulders. The sand was soft and at every step we sank down a couple of inches. I was close to fainting several times, and blood came out of my nose. The greatest problem was drinking water. Some days we had only one glass each of rotting water that we found by digging in the ground. One night three bears were 20 yards from Hasse, but somehow we managed to avoid them. We saw trails of jaguars every day—they call them tigers here.

Some areas we passed were surprisingly beautiful with tropical plants and an abundance of sea birds, pelicans, wading birds and herons. We saw alligators, some of them 20 feet long. In the ocean we spotted sharks, sawfish and dolphins. On the beach, many kinds of turtles. On land, opossums, raccoons and snakes, sometimes as thick as my leg, and up to 15 feet long. Sometimes we waded in swamps with water up to our waists, and alligators lurking around us.

Miami, January 12, 1872

We have left the Indians now, and I see that it is your birthday! How good it would have been to spend the evening with you! Good luck, dear Knut. Perhaps I will be home with you next winter. But right now I am sitting in a dilapidated, uninhabited house on the beach. Tonight we will begin our long journey back, as we are running out of money. I only have four small gold coins left, half of which I will need for renting a boat further up.

If only you were here, to see the golden sunset and feel the mild breeze. You would think you had been transported to a magic place. It is also dangerous and difficult. But I wish it was with you I had walked these 250 miles.

Your friend Josef

In March 1872, Josef's brother Esaias wrote to their father Lars, as always thanking him for his love and support. (Lars had always encouraged his children to pursue their dreams, and when needed, he also helped them financially.) Esaias told Lars that they were all healthy and the environment was lovely. The chickens had started to produce eggs, and they had bought a mule. They had work and food, and milk for Signe, the baby daughter of Wilhelm and Hanna. They were growing corn, beans and potatoes, and had planted orange trees around the house.

They had been worried about Josef and Bergman who had been gone for so long. Sofia had feared they were dead. But, late one evening they suddenly appeared—bearded, dirty, exhausted, their clothes torn and shoes worn out. Their journey had been incredible—everyone who heard about it was amazed. Esaias hoped the stories would be published some day...

Regarding Americans, Esaias remarked that they lie and boast, in a way that Swedish people seldom would. The newspapers were full of lies about the political parties. Most advertising for merchandise was false, as was the recruitment propaganda for immigrants. The pamphlets were painting a false picture of life in America. A few lucky settlers were hailed, but the majority, who had a hard time, were not mentioned.

In April Esaias wrote about a man named Thieman who had come over from Sweden with him and Wilhelm. This Thieman was unreliable and troublesome and was now being attacked in the papers. A newspaper clipping from a Savannah paper was enclosed. It stated that several Swedes had left their employers for mysterious reasons and had gone to parts unknown. Now somebody had called the newspaper saying the Swedes had been induced to leave by Rev. A. Thieman, and that they were staying in Thomasville.

Esaias was glad that they would soon get a new dock for steamships, a large new hotel, and possibly their own post office.

Other news, from May 1872, was that a friend of the brothers from Upsala University, Anders Aulin, had arrived. He was now staying with the Henschens. Henrik Lilljebjörn, Hanna's brother, who also lived with them, had proposed marriage to their twenty-year-old neighbor Miss Putnam. But since Henrik was only nineteen, she wouldn't have him! However, Henrik was working hard and doing well. Being underage, he didn't have to pay taxes.

By June 1872, the Swedes who had come with Wilhelm the year before, and who had stayed, were *now free workers and no longer indentured. Now they could start getting salaries. Esaias said that many of them went north, where they had relatives. They were also hoping to get better wages than the average $20 a month that Henry Sanford offered them. Andersson, the blacksmith, was offered $22, and Sanford would set up a smithy and tools for him. Andersson's wife would only get $8. Lindberg, the baker, was offered $30. Johansson, Almgren and Löfgren were negotiating with Sanford to get their families sent over from Sweden.*

Josef meanwhile had gone up the coast to Jacksonville. He had intended to return to Sweden to continue his medical studies, but his plans changed.

Letter 3 from Josef to Knut

Jacksonville, July 1872

My dear Knut!

It is now a few months since I wrote to you. I then wrote from Miami, the Indian (and usual) name of a place which the government calls Fort Dallas.

I would love to hear from you. If you don't want to write, please send me some news via Salomon. I wonder how you are doing this winter. Have you have been ill again? And what are you doing this summer? Your portrait is on my table and I look at it daily, but it is not the same as actually being with you and looking into your dark eyes. I would love to have you here and show you the forest and the palm trees. I would give you skulls of bears, foxes and raccoons. You should see the chameleon lizards—how they inflate themselves and change colors, and run and jump in the tree outside my window. They chase flies and insects. And you should see the 5 inch spiders which, with my full agreement, eat all the flying and crawling insects in my room. They move like shadows over the walls. You would be frightened, as I was in the beginning, but you would get used to them, just as I have. Now they are the most normal thing.

But I was going to tell you what happened on my way back from the Indians. Billie, a gloomy looking Indian, took Hasse and me down the Miami River in a canoe. We sat on the bottom, he stood at the back. With long strokes he pushed the canoe down the river. Sometimes it went fast like an arrow, sometimes slow. We tried to cheer Billie up with jokes and talk. He smiled when we tried to speak his Seminole language. Once in a while, when we managed to pronounce something correctly, he said: "Inko!"

The scenery around the river was the most beautiful tropical landscape I had ever seen. Cabbage and coconut palms, jungle and endless panoramas over the Everglades. Magnificent web-footed birds and waders and occasional alligators entertained us. In Miami we were able to get a ride with a group of people who were going to a funeral 8 miles up the coast. We changed boats several times. Bergman was a bit scared in the dark, but I wasn't. I could see that the kind Negro who steered the boat knew what he was doing. At 1:00 a.m. we arrived, unexpected and uninvited, at the house where the funeral would take place. We slept comfortably in the hall. Imagine my surprise, to find beautiful walnut furniture with velvet covering, tables with marble tops and an excellent library, in the middle of the jungle! Turned out we had come to the local judge, who is also the Senator of the County. The next day we were able to meet the host, who was dressed in black due to the funeral. We apologized for our clothing.

That was the first time in weeks I had been able to undress and sleep in a bed. I was very tempted to accept their generous offer to stay, have breakfast and come to the funeral. But we had a schedule to adhere to. Mr. Brown was supposed to meet us at the mouth of New River and take us across those deep, shark-infested waters. At 4:00 p.m. we had to be 20 miles away from where we were, and the day was getting hot. We asked a Negro who had come with us from Miami to get us across Biscayne Bay, which is the name of this bay. He took us on a boat, but did not know how to sail, and the boat was scruffy and leaking. It got quite windy, and he was frightened. I helped him sail, and somehow we progressed, though we got stuck on sand banks several times.

But where did he put us ashore? There was hardly a yard of land to stand on! It was the most terrible mess of broken and fallen mangrove and cypress forest, a leftover from the hurricane last August. I had never seen such devastation. The gigantic mangrove trunks were broken and split like straws. The damaged trees were leaning on the few trees that were still standing. This is how they will remain for decades, maybe centuries, until a new horrific hurricane will break down everything.

We fortified our courage and senses with crackers and cheese, and filled our bottles from Biscayne Bay, which to our astonishment had sweet water. This phenomenon must be due to the rivers and streams that come from the Everglades, and from the winds, since the bay is shallow.

The ocean was roaring on the other side of the strip of land which we had to traverse. I estimated the distance to 1 or 2 miles. I climbed up on a mangrove trunk. From my higher position I saw that there was no way we could walk on the ground, as there was water, mud, fallen trees and thicket everywhere. We had to traverse by "air", meaning we had to climb and cling to the crowns of trees, and use the fallen trees as bridges. Bergman sighed, and so did I. We put our luggage on our backs, and the water bottles and food packages over our shoulders. Then we started our tightrope walk. We had to balance our bodies and the 40 pounds we carried on our backs, and somehow make forward progress. I had to have my hands free to use my knife to check if the branches were healthy or decayed. When we look back at it, we are still amazed at how we made it. I wore "bulda" shoes, and Bergman wore "lapp" shoes, which made us more stable on our feet. Sometimes I had to crawl on hands and knees; sometimes I could walk straight, high in the sky on some huge tree trunk that had fallen diagonally onto an adjacent tree. Sometimes I sat down for a while, looking for a better way to progress. Sometimes we had to retreat a bit when it was impossible to go further. Sometimes I had to jump, and in one of my jumps a bottle broke and leaked all over my clothes. Later, when we walked on the white, burning sand, I missed that bottle bitterly. One of Bergman's bottles also broke.

Bergman followed me and did well, although I once had to go back and help him out of a bad spot. It is a pity we couldn't stay in the tree tops long enough for Bergman to make a drawing of the surroundings. But the sun rose higher and higher and we needed to get down from the trees. We felt like monkeys in a primeval forest, of the kind I had seen in books in my childhood. The view was sometimes magnificent.

Finally we were out of the mangrove and cypress forest. We now walked in saw palmetto and heard the waves more clearly. Our faces and hands were scratched up, but we kept walking briskly. The ground leaned upwards. I smelled salt water and then saw the beach and the ocean—hurrah! I finally felt I was on my way home. However, when I walked on the loose sand and the sun burned my neck, I sighed and panted. But could I refrain from collecting shells and sea beans? No! I filled all pockets and handkerchiefs with shells, corals and three hundred sea beans, which in their rough condition are worth $15-20.

We were hurrying desperately to try to make it to the mouth of New River at the agreed-upon time. Soon we realized this would be impossible. My shoes were broken and kept filling up with sand. Because of the time I lost by constantly emptying my shoes, Bergman advanced faster than I. The heat and thirst tortured us both, and we had long stopped talking to each other when we walked together. At one point I sat down on a tree trunk, took a break and had some food. Meanwhile Bergman disappeared before me.

Finally I removed my shoes and walked barefoot on the sand. The waves often came up to my knees, which cooled me off a bit. The thirst was the hardest. It was torture to see the clear water shine and glisten beside me, and not being able to drink it. Sometimes I wet my lips with it but the saltiness made me stop quickly.

About 4:00 or 5:00 p.m., I saw some figures far down the coast. Eventually I caught up with them and Bergman. It was Mr. Brown and his son, who kindly had waited for us and had walked 3 or 4 miles in our direction, to find us. They asked many questions, but my tongue was glued to my gums. I hurried to their boat to drink from their bottle.

Now I could see the sand banks that surrounded the mouth of the river, and the thousands of gulls and birds that covered them. I had my gun but was too exhausted to try to shoot them. After an hour in the boat we came to Brown's house where we received supper. We told all our adventures to the Brown family, and then finally went to sleep.

Your friend Josef

The same month, July 1872, while Josef was in Jacksonville, Wilhelm and Hanna had a new baby, Carl. He was the first Henschen child to be born in America. Hanna, Wilhelm and their two children now had their own household and would soon move to New York.

Esaias reported that most of the Swedes in Mellonville, both the free and the indentured, were generally happy and satisfied with Sanford.

By August 1872, Anders Aulin, who had changed his first name to Andrew, had been staying with Esaias for two months. They had known each other in Upsala, but now they had become close friends. Aulin was a pleasant and hard-working man. He had a good sense of humor and an inexhaustible stock of funny stories from their student days in Upsala. This helped to cheer up Esaias who was often depressed. The atmosphere in the house was very good, but Esaias said only God could truly help and console him.

Sofia had decided to stay in Florida (instead of moving up north with Wilhelm) and had joined the household of Esaias, Aulin and Henrik. The men made breakfast and Sofia cooked dinner.

Esaias missed the books, music and culture he used to enjoy in Sweden. He asked his father to send him magazines and literature from Sweden, and Aulin asked for Shakespeare's works in Swedish. Aulin's fiancée, who was supposed to come over from Sweden, was not coming after all. The next year, 1873, Aulin married one of their neighbor Lawton's daughters, Lona, instead. (Andrew Aulin would later give the town of Oviedo its name, and be its first postmaster.)

Lars Henschen was regularly trying to persuade his sons Josef and Esaias to get married. But Josef hadn't found any girl he liked, and neither had Esaias who was still torn between love of women and love of God. Also, both Josef and Esaias were still very poor and would not have been able to support wives.

Sofia wrote to Lars, who was her first cousin and beloved friend. She told him she was healthy and happy because God gave her strength. They all lived a peaceful life together in love and trust. There were no fights or suspicions. Josef was now back from Jacksonville and had re-joined their household. He had built a chicken pen for Sofia. She had twenty-six newborn chicks and twenty-one adult hens. Soon they would start laying eggs. Sofia was planning to sell the eggs to add to her income.

Otto Fries, another friend from Upsala, had arrived in Jesup and was now staying with them. (The Fries family in Sweden was related to the Ångströms.) Otto was very nice and they were all glad to have him.

By October 1872, Hanna and Wilhelm had moved to New York. Josef, Esaias and their friends were growing cabbage and also watermelons which they could sell for 50 cents each. Sofia needed glasses, Josef needed shoes. Could Father please send such items? And matches, which they needed constantly and were so expensive in Florida.

In November 1872, Henry Sanford, who was often abroad, visited Mellonville. He was making decisions about getting the families of his workers over to Florida. Some of the wives would now finally come.

Sometimes the Swedes had chills and fever. Otto Fries at one point was very ill and delirious, and so was Esaias. Almgren was ill for four months and almost died. They thought he was dead, washed his body and carried him off to be buried. Then he suddenly woke up! Now he was well again.

Lars had been talking about visiting his sons in Florida. They told him they would love to have him, but he wouldn't like the diet—pork and potatoes was all they had to eat.

Letter 4 from Josef to Knut

Lake Jesup, January 13, 1873

Dear Knut,

Another year has gone by. Yesterday was your birthday. I guess you were celebrating with your friends. How I would have loved to be in the group and rejoice with you. I think it is your sixteenth birthday. But of one thing I am sure—in a few months it will be ten years since that Sunday morning when a small child appeared in my lab and immediately won my affection. I hope you have not forgotten it, despite the fact that I have not heard a word from you since I left Sweden. I hope it is temporary. I do wish you luck with your new year. May your health keep improving, and not be damaged by the terrible winters at home. Let me know in which grade you are, what subjects you enjoy the most, and if you have any nice friends. Is there still crust on the snow? We have heard that the winter at home has been mild for quite a while.

On August 26, 1871, a few months before I arrived, there was a great storm here, as great as the one you had in Sweden. It was not as devastating here as in Sweden, because there is so little habitation in Florida. However, it did throw ships up on land, and it tore down homes. Last winter in Jacksonville we had a tornado, a twister, which swept away houses and trees. A woman was blown up into a high pine tree and had to be rescued with long ladders. Another person was unfortunate enough to be blown into the river and drown.

I made an enjoyable trip to New Smyrna by the sea, just before Christmas. Our caravan looked like a gang of gypsies with women, children, pots, fishing and hunting gear, barrels, pillows, blankets, and food. It took us two days to cover 50 miles. We traveled across rivers and creeks, through forests, prairies and cypress swamp. Hunting was good. One evening I went down to Mosquito River (a salt water lagoon). There I saw a fin move, and thought it was a shark, but then it looked more like a porpoise. I hesitated about shooting because it seemed to be small and insignificant, and the distance was great. But the temptation was too strong. I shot. The water soared up high and got colored by blood. I threw off my clothes and waded out, with my hunting knife in my hand, not sure what I was going to find. What did I see if not a huge otter who tried to bite me, although he was seriously injured. My attempts to strangle him failed, because his neck was enormously thick. To not damage the fur, I smothered him under the water. It was the largest otter the people here had ever seen. The skin has now been dried (not stretched) and is 4 feet, or twice as big as the European otter. These furs are worth $4 to $5. Unfortunately the pigs ate his head. This fur, if not eaten by insects or rats, will be sent to Upsala. Tonight I will stuff a deer head, and am sorry I don't have the arsenic and green soap I need.

You have probably heard about the smell of a skunk. On the prairie, on the way to Smyrna, the dogs started to bark. We couldn't see what they were barking at, but supposed it was a polecat. I got out my gun and ran through the grass towards it. I saw a small animal with a bushy tail standing straight up, which stood there calmly and now and then jumped towards the dogs, who fearfully retreated. Around the animal I perceived an intense onion-like smell. I shot it and brought it back to the carriage. At home I skinned it, and made a careful autopsy. While doing so, I accidentally got sprayed with the liquid from its gland. After that I had ample opportunity to enjoy the stink. I am considering dipping some papers in the liquid and sending them to my zoologist friends in Upsala. But I think the letters would be discarded by the postal workers on the way. In spite of constant washing, the smell permeated my hands for two weeks, and a small piece of meat that had been forgotten polluted the air in my house for a long time. When I finished the autopsy job by the evening, I tried to go to bed as usual, next to Otto Fries. But he started to scream, and Henrik and Esaias threw me out of the house.

However, it is not true that the smell never goes away. After a few weeks, having hung my coat outside to air out, it was completely odorless and I could use it again. I think I now can stand any smell. Nobody down here could stand skinning a polecat. We have two kinds of them, the larger (Mephitis Chinga) which is the one I wrote about, and the smaller (M. Zorilla) slightly larger than a squirrel, with white stripes, lively and handsome. I have seen that one in southern Florida but never shot one. We also have varieties of Felis Coneolor and F. Ruva (American lynx). They are called catamounts. A Negro shot one while I was gone. Esaias saw it and said it looked like a mix of cougar and wildcat. Apart from Felis Onca, these are the only ones known to live here. They are not uncommon!

Now in the winter we have all the birds from the north here—swallows, larks, thrushes, fly-catchers, finches. Ducks are swimming in the forest lakes, and wading birds are walking around everywhere in the swamps and marshes. There was tremendous chirping and quacking in a cypress marsh that I passed the other day. I had to stop to enjoy it. I couldn't bring myself to shoot the beautiful little birds, although I would have liked to examine some of the unusual ones. They shimmered in the magnificent colors of the South. Some of the more modest ones from the North were also present. Then a group of jubilant parrots arrived. Green with yellow heads and necks, they descended at the end of the marsh with terrific chatter. They were fairly timorous. In the mornings and evenings they fly around the river, and sometimes descend close to our house.

Two weeks ago I rode over to Lake Conway, 20 miles away, together with Mr. St. John, an Englishman. We encountered hordes of long legged cranes, which were incredibly noisy. They marched in a regular rhythm and were not afraid of us. I caught one of these alive on my way to Smyrna, and an American killed it for me.

The oranges here cost about the same as Swedish potatoes, $3.50 per barrel. Esaias and Otto Fries are planting the seeds, and we eat a lot of them every day. Fries is letting people eat them for free as long as they return the seeds to him. I bet you wouldn't mind having this opportunity! The oranges here are much juicier and sweeter than the ones at home. 5 acres, planted with 1000–1100 orange trees, give a yearly income of

$10,000. They are planted on scrubland, the least fatty soil you can find here. Until the trees are fully grown, they need careful nursing. The Swedish workers who came with me immediately bought oranges and planted the seeds, and they now have several thousand plants. Each worker has received $125 worth of land as gifts, and may take more land on a ten-year credit. My brother Wilhelm has a beautiful orchard around his house, but while the trees are growing he is up in his New York office, where he makes $1200 a year. Esaias handles his plantation and is about to start one for himself as well. If one has relatives and friends here it is not hard to thrive, because the soil is good and the climate marvelous, except for a few frosty winter nights.

I wish I could entertain you with some funny adventure stories, but I haven't had any for a while. Well, one night I got lost in the jungle, walked in a circle, but that is not unusual around here. I have been living here peacefully since the autumn, helping my brothers, cutting, digging, building. But, after I have completed a court case with an American on February 1ˢᵗ, I want to leave. Don't know where I am going, just further out in the world.

This American owes me money, and I can't retrieve it without a trial. But I know I will win. We have decided to show the Americans that we understand their laws, and that they will not succeed in tricking us. A few have tried—you really have to be alert and watch your money. They are nice, open and pleasant to be around, but while being extremely friendly, they can cheat you thoroughly if you aren't careful. Wilhelm got badly duped in the beginning, but now we have become too smart for them. Some of the worst ones, who poisoned and killed their neighbor's pigs, ours as well, became meek as lambs when we told them we were starting a vigilance committee to drive them out of the area. They are given one month to sell their property and leave the area. If they are spotted here after that, they will be hanged from the nearest tree. This is the American method, undeniably effective. A jury will never convict you for such an execution. A large part of the well-known Ku Klux Klan crimes are actually retaliations against Negro criminals who in South Carolina, Alabama etc. are abundant and wild. The most atrocious crimes were committed by some Negroes, but they were protected by Grant's soldiers, as Grant needed the Negro votes for his re-election. I have talked to some Ku Kluxers, decent people, who told me they were completely exposed to the caprices of the Negroes after the war. The only way they could protect themselves was to frighten the blacks by hanging the worst criminals. Many things in this world look different when you see them close up.

Foreigners however can live here peacefully, unless they get mixed up in politics. I saw a funny election for City Council, last spring in Jacksonville. The Negroes beat their opponents with sticks, until they fled. Then they elected their City Council, half black, half Grant's clerks. A group of blacks had been pulled in from the countryside, enticed with brandy, and made to vote, although they didn't have the slightest right to do so. It was Grant's clerks who organized all this. What would people in Upsala say about such an election? Even here, people were amazed.

Please write to me! You can give a letter to Salomon, or send it to Jesup, as it will be forwarded to me. My best regards to your parents and sister.

Your special friend Josef

In March 1873 Esaias wrote to his father that they all still lived together in harmony. He knew that his father worried about his and Josef's interrupted studies at the university, but Esaias admitted that he had actually never liked to study. Josef did not miss his university studies either. He would soon move out to run a mill.

Letter 5 from Josef to Knut

Lake Maitland, April 13, 1873

Dear Knut,

I was thrilled to receive a letter from you! You have done a good deed, when you wrote this letter. There are not many true friends in the world; I noticed that before I left Sweden, and now more than ever I can't afford to lose them.

I hope your health will improve every year and that the cruel "Caesar" (*Knut's Latin teacher*) doesn't contribute to ruining it. I agree with you—not only is he cruel and tough but also highly *selfish*, and that I can't stand. It did help me considerably to learn French and especially English in school, but the way they teach you in Sweden is designed to make you hate to study. We could have learned these subjects in half the time if the teacher had been pleasant and used a good method.

Still, persist in your studies, and find some funny or interesting stories about the time periods you read about in your Latin class. That will help to keep your interest up, even though a lot of what we learn in school is useless.

I still have my old love for the natural sciences and still study them here, but I have changed my methods. I do miss the library. All scientific books are very expensive here—for example a Flora of the southern states costs $4.50!

There are plenty of opportunities here for a botanist or zoologist. The riches of Florida have hardly been studied at all. Even in the United States they are almost unknown. The springs of the Nile are better known by scientists than the St. Johns River. But, if someone wants to come here to study or research, he has to bring money for his living expenses. If you should want to come here one winter, I hope to be in a position to offer you a pleasant home and a good deal of experiences and advice. I have traveled around so much by now, that I know a fair amount about people and conditions, and I know the land and the roads (forest trails). How great it would be if you, instead of going to Vienna this year, would come to the event in Philadelphia in 1875. Then you would spend the winter with me in Florida, and after that I would return to Sweden with you. I am sorry to tell you that unless something unexpected happens, I will stay in Florida for the time being. I miss my friends in Upsala, but I don't miss Sweden. The delightful climate here has really enthralled me. It is wonderful to live in perpetual summer. If only I had more friends and books here, I wouldn't miss anything.

You say that Salomon is strangely silent about me, and you wish to know what I am doing. No surprise that he is silent, because I have been nothing more than a tourist. The only business I have attempted is photography, but unfortunate circumstances, like losing some of my luggage in New York, made me unable to get a good start on that. So I packed up my stuff and planned to go into some other business in New York or the northern states.

I received a general job offer from the Lake Superior Railway in Minnesota, but as I suspected, they wanted to make me a land agent. I didn't want to be that, because I didn't know if I could offer the land with a good conscience, and also I don't like to freeze, any more than I liked it in Sweden.

I was in Jacksonville, ready to go to New York (*and from there back to Sweden*), and went looking for a porter who could take my things to the steamship. But I had forgotten that it was Sunday. Not even the black people wanted to work, although I offered them triple payment. In England and America people are funny about the Sunday. They live in sin six days a week, and on the seventh day they imagine they have become righteous as long as they don't work that day.

The people who poison the animals of their poor neighbors one day are preaching about God the next day, criticizing the Swedes because they took their guns and went into the forest to hunt on a Sunday afternoon.

I got so annoyed about missing my boat that I boarded the next steamer, one that went south instead of north. I ended up in Jesup again, with my relatives. I was only going to stay a short time, but became ill—probably because I had walked 20 miles in the scorching sun, with a heavy backpack, and fasting. I make little mistakes like that sometimes. Had to stay two weeks in Jesup. When I was well I gave up the idea of going to New York, and started to work with various things. I cut down some cedars, as I knew I could sell them for between 50 cents and $1 per cubic foot. The forest was full of animal life. I went out early in the morning, with my lunch in a tin bucket, and sang while I was cutting. I rested under the palm trees and had my lunch by a creek. Parrots and squirrels kept me company. When I walked home in the evenings (about 2 miles) I encountered raccoons, polecats, opossums and owls. I was happy and joyful as a clam and really got a taste for this kind of life. The thrushes and warblers sang jubilantly and I heard woodpeckers as well.

When I was ready to take my lumber to Jacksonville, the Englishman Mr. St. John visited one night, and casually mentioned that a sawmill with cotton-cleaning machines was free to hire. I thought about it all night, and in the morning I told Mr. St. John: "If you can stay one more day, I will go with you and take that mill, if you think I can get it—today I have to work on public roads." (Everybody has to do that if they stay 14 days in a county.) He said: "Mr. Holden, the owner, will be glad to have you."

That was how I got the mill. I am running this business alone, and pay half the net income as my lease. Now I have workers here and we repair the mill house and will rebuild the dams and raise the waterfall to ten feet.

I have my own household now, even if not a home. There is an abundance of fish, turtles and wildlife here. The second day we shot a large trout. It is a delicious fish. The turtles crawl up on land and are easy to catch. Large herds of deer roam just a few miles from the mill. The water that runs the mill comes from a number of lakes surrounded by pine and deciduous forests. The lake above us is one of the most beautiful little lakes in Florida, about 2 or 3 miles long with pretty little islets and capes. It is a mile from the mill so I don't have a view of it. It is called Lake Maitland, and there is a post office on the other side of it. I have to walk 3 miles around the lake to get to it.

Below the mill is another pretty lake, Lake Howell, of which I do have a view. This one is also about 2 miles long but has a more rounded shape. The creek between these two lakes spreads out into swamps, tightly covered with bushes and ponds in the middle.

April 14. There are innumerable water birds here; herons, cranes, ducks, water turkeys etc. The white herons have plumes that you can sell for $5 each. One person earned $500 in two weeks by shooting these herons. Among the fish we have half-pound salmon, trout, perch, carp etc. I just had a fat salmon for dinner.

At night I hear the alligators grumble in the stream and sometimes I see them swim in Lake Howell. Water snakes are also common. We have already killed four or five in two weeks. One of them, the Moccasin Snake, is poisonous.

It is a strange view when the sun shines on the stream. The bottom is white sand, and the water is slightly brownish but still clear. We can see the fish swim and rush for the stickleback and small crabs. Sometimes a small turtle crawls on the bottom. You see it the most clearly when the evening sun throws slanted rays through the water. It is like a small aquarium, where not even the small Vallisneria Spiralis is missing. It thrives everywhere in Florida's sweet waters. The depth of the creek varies from one foot to seven feet. There is plenty of water. The stream below the mill is very narrow when the mill is dammed up, and small oaks grow around it. Spanish Moss hang from their branches, swinging in the wind. It is excellent for stuffing mattresses and is very similar to horsehair. They are made wet, and pounded, so that only black threads remain. We collected several large bags in a few hours.

My home is a simple frame house of stilts, bolts and lumber. It is divided into two rooms with a chimney in the middle which opens up to both rooms with a big fireplace for each. Sometimes we make a fire and sit by it and talk. Sometimes Americans come here to get something ground, or to buy lumber, and then they tell their adventure stories from California, Mexico, Peru and around the world. It is not unusual to meet simple men who have traveled more than the rich people at home. The life of the Americans, here on the border of civilization, is full of adventures. Casually and eloquently they describe the most terrifying dangers. They are cheerful, have a good sense of humor, and we always listen with interest to a good story. The Indian wars, which are still going on, the war with Mexico, the Rebellion of 1862-67, digging for gold in California, hunting adventures, all these make good stories. Sometimes they tell you about some nasty deed they have done—their ethics level doesn't seem to be very high. It is the "smart" person who is always most admired.

You wanted to know what I am doing. I could be called a mill owner, but I am participating in the work. I work in the forest; I grind grain for customers, and many other things. Right now my four workers are having their siesta. I give them a two hour lunch break. This morning I built structures in the water, in order to put a floor under the water behind the mill. All this work I did myself, as our dear Swedes are afraid to get wet. I am the builder—here you have to be willing to do anything. Once I have everything set up and have grooved in the workers in sawing, grinding, cleaning cotton etc. I don't plan to be stuck in the mill. I will travel around, take orders, find customers and expand the business. I have also become an agent for Anchor Line Steamers and can sell tickets from New York to various places in Europe, where the large steamers go. It would be easy to make a ticket to Trieste, and from there take the train to Vienna to meet you, if I didn't have to send the payment to the main office in New York. I can also sell tickets from the best places in Europe, to New York. This is no big business down here in the woods, but I make a few dollars. I get 10% of the money paid for tickets. A bunch of Swedish boys will be sending for girlfriends, of that I am sure.

Also, I intend to do business with sewing and knitting machines and other household machines and carpentry items from a factory up north. This year the profit will not be great, but I hope it will improve. And if it doesn't, I will leave it and do something else. That is completely acceptable here. In Jacksonville I saw a man who was a photographer one day and a saddle maker the next. "My business didn't pay," he said calmly.

I am telling you all this because you are my friend, but I would like it to stay just between us. I have never done anything I am ashamed of, and never will, but you know that conditions and prejudices are different back home in Sweden from what they are here.

I still have my old interests and in my spare time I make cages for parrots, mockingbirds, squirrels etc. Soon I will make a pond for fish and turtles so I can study their habits. I want to have a nice environment. Accumulating money is not a great interest for me, I am happy if I have the essentials. I have a puppy of a race so large that he already can put his head on the table. He will be a good watch dog, because my neighbors are not particularly friendly. For years they had made their living from the mill and cheated the owner out of all his income. They are furious that I have put an end to all that. First they didn't want to turn the mill over to me. I sent for the owner, a meek kind of man, who rather suffers than tells someone off. In his presence, I told the guys how they had been defrauding the owner, and that this would now stop. They were shaking with anger, but the result was that I got the right to run the mill, which they didn't have the faintest right to. If they would have made more trouble, I would have taken them to court. After they gave up the mill they became nice and polite and one of them asked me to employ him! I didn't give him an answer. Since then he has twice been stealing in the mill, one time tools, one time lumber. I forced him to return the lumber. I don't have proof about the tools, but one day I will hide and catch him red-handed and send him to jail, which is in Chattahoochee in northern Florida.

There are plenty of crooks here in America, but there are also quick ways to get rid of them. In the beginning we were shy and polite, but that doesn't work with the crooks. Now we are more experienced, and I am trying to gain respect for the Swedes. I have sued three persons who tried to cheat Swedes out of their salaries, and have won all three court cases. The property of one of the crooks will be sold any day now. We have also scared a few other racketeers, so that they don't dare to do any more tricks.

It is funny to observe Americans. The worse I treat them, the more polite they become. But if I am polite and meek myself, they start taking liberties. Now I have told you lots of bad things about Americans, but actually there are plenty of decent people among them. Those are nice to associate with. There is just one problem; you can't make any real friends, because as soon as interests collide, it is the end of the friendship. This is something that is hard to accept, and may eventually be a reason for me to return to Sweden.

You must keep up the correspondence with me, because it is a great pleasure to get letters from you. Tell me some details from your life. It is the details that make me better able to imagine your life. The big, serious events are good to hear, but between us, the small incidents are more interesting. I get a weekly newspaper from Chicago, which tells me both what has happened and what hasn't happened.

I have lost 35 pounds; all of my fat is gone. My muscles have increased and my calves now measure 17 inches around them. My health is good and my mood OK. I still joke a lot, but I can't help getting older, and my jokes now are more to entertain others, not myself. I hope I will never become grumpy, even if I become an old recluse. Two women have proposed to me, a widow and a young lady, but I am not interested in them.

April 16. The temperature is +27 Celsius at 1 p.m., and was +20 this morning. A fresh wind is blowing and it feels fairly cool. My workers are taking their siesta and I am sitting here, imagining that I am talking to you.

My four bulls escaped last night and are probably walking towards Orlando, where they come from. There are no fences to stop them, even if they keep walking to Chicago or to the Arctic Ocean. One of my men has been looking for them all day.

I am making a railway on both sides of the mill so that I can transport my products. Next week I will build a little smithy.

In an American newspaper I read that your father received the Rumsford Medal and some money as well. It annoyed me though, that they said he was German. There was a good description of the latest discoveries in Spectrum Analysis and of its founder. Apart from the error of calling him German, and spelling his name Angstrom instead of Ångström, he was fully credited and admired.

Your devoted friend Josef

Letter 6 from Josef to Knut

Lake Maitland, May 1, 1873

Dear Knut,

I hope you had a happy Walpurgis Night (*traditional Swedish celebration of spring*). I would have liked to be there with you, to see the students march up to the castle.

No special news here. I got up at 5:30 a.m. Looked after my parrot and turtles to make sure they were comfortable. At 6:00 I presided at the breakfast table, served coffee to my five workers etc. 6:15 we started working on the canal from the mill. Lunch and siesta 12:00-2:00, then back to work. Some of us fell in the canal and there was lots of laughter. The sun went down 6:30, and at 7:00 we stopped working. Thick clouds were gathering. Dinner was corn pudding, corn bread, coffee without cream, and fresh wheat buns. Then we chatted about Upsala and the students marching and making Walpurgis speeches. And now the Lord is making a speech right here, making the house shake. A tropical thunderstorm is raging, rain cascading. Martin Andersson is sitting next to me, reading the Bible. From the next room I hear the Negro doing spelling exercises in the ABC book. You are probably asleep, and I soon will be too.

Your friend Josef

In July 1873 Esais mentioned to his father that a Swede named Månsson, currently living in Illinois, was visiting him. This Månsson, who seemed to have Americanized his name to Munsen, was tired of the cold winters up north and was thinking of settling in Jesup. If he would, many of his Swedish friends from Illinois would join him here. Esaias wasn't sure if a new Swedish colony in the area would be a curse or a blessing, but meanwhile he was hospitable to his guest. Månsson said that he in any case was going back to his city of birth in Sweden in the fall, and would bring back a number of friends and neighbors to America.

In September Esaias wrote that he was tired of the unchanging Florida diet, and longed for an anchovy sandwich and other customary food he used to eat in Upsala. Esaias said his neighbors went hunting, and could thus vary their diet with deer meat. But Esaias didn't hunt and had no deer meat. The neighbors were drinking coffee with every meal, Esaias only one cup in the morning, because it was too expensive.

Lotta, a girl who came from Sweden in 1871, was about to marry the baker Lindberg. Otto Fries was expecting his family to come over soon.

Sofia needed money for bed linen, and especially for clothes and shoes. Otherwise she would walk around in torn clothes and bare feet. This actually applied to all of them, but was unusual among white women. In the spring when there was no money, Sofia, sixty-eight years old, had to walk barefoot.

"Black people have a good future in central Florida, judging from my limited experience" Esaias wrote in September 1873. "Many buy land and plantations and save up their earnings. The whites run a Sunday school for them, teaching them reading, writing and biblical history. Eight or nine blacks are members of the local Baptist congregation. Apart from sermons and Sunday school, there are also non-denominational prayer meetings three times a week. Anyone can come and pray. It is hard to believe that people who were slave owners only ten years ago, have humbled themselves to give "the right hand of Christian fellowship" to any Negroes who wish to join the congregation. Even those who used to be strongly prejudiced against other races now seem to believe in every person's equality under God. One day, when the head of the congregation asked if any *of the brothers wanted to read the prayer, a black man stood up. When he started the usual introduction "Let us pray" all the blacks and whites, men and women, fell to their knees. The Negro completed the prayer, simply and properly. The colored people are currently negotiating with Aulin to get him as a school teacher. They will pay him well."*

"Since the blacks now are citizens with rights to vote, the whites are interested in educating them, so that they will not become pawns in the hands of party people from the North. And all working people have a mutual interest to see the state finances handled in an honest way, and to lessen the taxes."

"Even South Carolina, the state with the most preju-dice, has established free schools for blacks. According to the newspapers, the Catholics are proselytizing eagerly among the blacks. The Protestants do not want to leave the blacks in ignorance, making them easy prey for Catholics, who would surely use their votes, which to-gether with the Irish would be considerable."

"Experience shows that the Negroes have natural talents to be good farmers and craftsmen as long as they get some education."

These were Esaias' viewpoints...

Letter 7 from Josef to Knut

Maitland, January 25, 1874

My dearest boy,

Sunday morning and I was just sitting down to write to you, when the door flew up. I have no locks on my doors, just little wooden latches which now went to pieces in the storm.

I am cooking a pigs head for dinner. How strange my life is here, compared to life in Sweden. Here, you can't do much if your maid decides to walk out on you.

This morning my black maid informed me that she was leaving, for Orlando (our borough and district court) and wasn't sure when she was coming back. While I went to check on the stew, the rooster flew in, up on the table, and turned my ink bottle over—as you can see in my letter.

When the food was ready I hooted in my oxhorn, the usual signal to my men for dinner. Nobody came, so I had to go out on the roads to find them. After walking half a mile I found one of my guys, Almgren, who was dreaming about orange trees that he would plant on 160 acres. I am helping him get these acres from the government. After dinner I rode out in the forest, on my horse Jack. I ran into Miss Kedney, a young lady from Minnesota. Behind Jenny (Miss Kedney's horse), her aunt was walking, an old, infirm, but handsome lady. Miss Kedney's brother was walking with her.

Miss Kedney and I rode off together for a while. Just as the young ladies at home drop their handkerchiefs, Miss Kedney dropped her riding-whip, to test the agility of my back. Then I was invited for dinner, which the young lady herself prepared. After dinner we were telling stories, which I concluded with a spine-tingling ghost story from Sweden. It was a pleasant Sunday. I rode home in the moonlight.

It is tough to be a single man here, and unmarried men are uncommon. But I will not marry just to get a cook. Many girls here marry at the age of twelve! There are plenty of girls in all the older families, but even if they were starving, they would not go out and work. Even if they were treated like hostesses in the homes, which they often are.

Let me tell you about my horse Jack. In the week before Christmas I realized that it is good to have a horse. I scraped my last cents together and borrowed some more money, and drove off with my brother's mule and carriage. I camped by the St. Johns River, 23 miles from here, and crossed the river by ferry the next day. My destination was the St. Augustine area, 100 or 150 miles from my home, where there are vast salt water swamps. Wild horses are nursed there, and can be bought for $60-100. My intention was to then go to Mr. Browner and trade in the horse for three excellent oxen, which I need for driving the lumber to the mill.

My carriage and mule got stuck in the swamp—the water went up into the carriage and up to the back of the mule. It took considerable effort to get them out. After a while I found a canal, which had been started before the civil war, to lead the St. Johns River into the ocean, 200 miles from its mouth. I followed the canal until I came to a shallow place where I could cross. Then I crossed the prairie to the pine forest, where I ran into a bunch of half-wild pigs. Beautiful palm trees and live oaks bordered the forest. There was no road, but I found tracks of wheels, no more than two weeks old. I followed the tracks along the forest, and by dinnertime I found myself by a large, dense cypress swamp. I stopped to make food—ham and corn bread.

I rode for many hours, got lost several times, and had to turn around. On the prairie I passed an abandoned hut. Near it was a box, the size of a cigar box, marked "U.S. Mail." In the old days, the mail man would put letters here for the settler.

By nightfall I suddenly saw a light in the forest. Soon I was under the roof of a Mr. Fulls. Although his hut was poor and scruffy, he gave me a clean, comfortable bed in a small side room, completely built of lumber that had been hand-cut from cypress trees. The accommodations and breakfast cost me half a dollar.

One of Mr. Fulls' sons was also going to Smyrna the next day. I offered him a ride in my carriage, as the path through the jungle was very difficult.

On the way we met two German Jews, who thought I was one of them, because of my fair complexion and reddish beard. I hadn't spoken German for a long time, and it got mixed up with English.

By twilight we arrived at Mr. Bryan by the well known "Turnbull Swamp," or "Hammock," which stretches for 40 miles along the coast. It grows on a coral reef which is sometimes only covered by a foot of rich soil. There were high palm trees, giant live oaks, hickory etc. and hundreds of thousands of wild orange trees. No human hand had touched this tropical jungle for a hundred years. Then, this area was a huge magnificent orchard of oranges, lemons, limes, olives, grapes, almond trees, indigo etc. When the land was returned to Spain everything deteriorated and the settlers left the area. The Indians retrieved the land of their ancestors.

Mr. Bryan tried to persuade me to take on some land there, and it was tempting. His orchard was bearing fruit only four years after it was planted. If you own 100 mature orange trees here, you are financially independent. Bryan makes $1-2000 a year, without having to work much. But it is an enormous job to clear this kind of forest. If you settle on pine land instead, you have to wait longer for the fruit, but you have less initial work and cost. There is a Captain Swift in Turnbull Swamp who cuts down oaks for the U.S. Navy. He has 300 workers and 150 pairs of oxen, and his own steamboat on the lagoon. His daily expenses are $2-3000 and last year he made $100,000 in pure profit. He pays a simple lumberjack $25 a month. One who is able to broad-axe gets $40 a month, plus plenty of good food.

Mr. Bryan was very hospitable and I stayed overnight. The next day (the 22nd, my birthday), after considerable bargaining, I bought a pony from him, for $110 in cash. I named him Jack—he is the size of a Swedish farm horse. I also bought 100 wild orange trees for 10 cents each, or rather exchanged my large revolver for them. As you see, all the stuff I brought from Sweden is coming in handy. I bought this revolver cheaply at an auction in Stockholm, and now I was glad I had it to trade. (My saddle and bridle, which I brought from Sweden, have been very useful and are already worn out by my brothers.) I dug up 40 orange trees and took them home, the rest will have to wait for later.

On my way home I passed five or six men on horses who were chasing half-wild cattle. Sometimes a cow would stray from the herd and then three or four guys rushed off to find it. I got lost several times, and almost despaired, but finally made it back to Lake Jesup. On the main road I saw a tiger cat—a catamount.

When I came home I heard a pig screaming terribly in the forest. I could tell from the screams that a bear was attacking it. Next day we found the bear tracks. There are plenty of pigs here which live on acorns and hickory nuts, but the bears are also numerous and often eat the pigs.

Please write soon to your loving friend Josef

Letter 8 from Josef to Knut

Lake Maitland, Orange County, July 19, 1874

My dearest Knut,

It was with deep sadness and concern I recently heard from Otto Fries that your health is still bad. I hope that you, or one of your family members, will let me know how you are doing. I hope it is nothing serious. Don't study too hard! I know you are highly ambitious, which is admirable, but don't let it ruin your health! If your health gets damaged early, it will be a heavy burden for the rest of your life. I hope you will not be offended that I speak my mind like this. You know, that I care for you greatly, and that your sparkling eyes were always a source of joy for me when I saw you in Sweden.

Dear Knut, postpone your exams a bit, and make a serious effort to improve your health. I know that your parents are willing to pay any costs needed for this.

I have bought some new land 1.5 miles from where I am now. Since I last wrote I have spent a lot of time on the mill, but I am not making much money on it, as it is old and worn and needs frequent repairs. I realize that it is much more lucrative to maintain my orange grove and expand it. So now I will call myself a plantation owner instead of a builder. My contract with the mill runs out August 15.

My land contains 161 acres, of which 20 acres are in the Lake Maitland. The land is mainly pineland of the best kind. Only one acre has deciduous trees, and half an acre is useless bush-covered land. The pine trees (Pinus Australis) are fairly sparse, (which makes it easy to clear the land) but they are tall and handsome with their 15- to18-inch needles in large bunches or brooms. They are similar to the large pines in Upsala. When I hear the rush of the wind through their crowns, I dream about Sweden, about hiking in Dalarna or Uppland (*Swedish counties*). Ah, there is music in the wind, whether it breezes in the tree tops or shakes our houses.

The soil is very sandy, covered with grass. All the types of grass can be burnt—we burn the ground every year, and the grass comes right back. In the spring, after a burning, this fine grass immediately shoots up and covers the area, a real joy to look at. Many flower also come up, and although I have walked around here quite a lot, I keep discovering new magnificent flowers.

My land is in a good location—near a general store, post office, mill and church. I will build my home by the beautiful Lake Maitland and will have a lovely view over the lake. I just need some more palm trees and tropical plants—then it will be perfect. I will try to move a few palms and plant them by my house. I wish I could describe the magic of the moonlight on the lake—that alone is worth a visit to Florida!

About my orange plantation. First you clear and burn the forest, then you plough the soil or break it up with a hoe, if it is full of roots like by Jesup. The most difficult ones are the long roots of the saw palmetto, but

I don't have too much of them. Then you plant your orange seedlings, which should be at least three years old. They have to be 25-33 feet apart, as their crowns will cover all the space between them. In an old orchard there are very enjoyable shaded walks. You can put 60-75 trees on an acre. A wild, grafted tree bears fruit in four or five years, and when fully grown it yields 1000-2000 oranges per year. Old, large trees can give up to 10,000. You can understand how lucrative this is, since oranges are paid 2 cents each, and shipped to New York 5 cents. After deduction of costs (ploughing, fertilizing and packaging of the fruit) your profit from 100 trees is $1000-2000, and that is quite a bit of wealth. Thousands of people come here to try their luck with this, but many leave with big losses, because they didn't understand or care what kind of soil to choose, or how to maintain the trees etc. A lot of people who come here have no experience with farming or fruit trees. Some arrive with money, some arrive with nothing.

Among the latest arrivals is an ex-rebel general Sturdivant from Alabama with his family, among them a good-looking daughter who still has no suntan on her face. He arrived by land with two wagons, looking for a while for the best land, before settling here. Now they are camping in a tent while building their house. They often come to the mill for lumber. The general, a plump and jolly man, is driving his own mules now, instead of having his soldiers do it, as during the war.

My closest neighbor and best friend among the Americans is Mr. Kedney, who used to be an Admiral's secretary in the U.S. Navy. He is a good-humored chap, always making jokes, but hard-working and practical. His orange orchard is the best in the area.

I have just come back from a trip to St. Augustine, 300 miles back and forth. My little pony, whom I bought just before Christmas, escaped after two months. I must have gone 500 miles looking for him in St. Augustine. This town is America's oldest settlement with a fort from the time when the Spaniards were here. (Skeletons in chains have been found locked into hidden arches.) In the town there are many descendants of the Spaniards, dark skinned and dark eyed. The girls are beautiful. They live in Spanish style homes with balconies etc. It is an interesting little town.

Thank you for the handsome portrait that Mrs. Fries brought over. You look well fed and healthy on it.

My best regards to your father, mother and sister and future brother in law, from your special devoted friend Josef

In June 1874, Knut's father, Anders Jonas Ångström, died after a short illness, only sixty years old. Knut was seventeen and had had his own health problems— probably tuberculosis—for many years. He sent a letter to Josef.

Letter 9 from Josef to Knut

Maitland, August 3, 1874

My dearest Knut,

I am sending you my deepest, most sincere condolences regarding your father's death. Now that I hear it from you I understand it is true—I couldn't believe it when I first heard it a week ago from a friend of Esaias who just arrived.

My dear boy, now you are suddenly and unexpectedly fatherless at a young age. I wish I could be by your side to console you and share your sorrow. But you have a better consoler, if you trust in Him! He has promised to be the friend of the fatherless.

For me, your father was first and foremost *your father* and I usually only thought of him as such. But as anyone who is interested in science, I rejoiced in his discoveries, and as a Swede I was proud of his successes and awards. *You* have therefore twice the reason to love and honor your father's memory, and I will be glad to hear you talk about him in your letters. You show me the greatest trust when you write to me about the things you most love to talk about.

Your father passed away in the bloom of his life, and it is a great loss for science and for his loved ones. What was best for *him* we cannot judge, but we have to believe that what happened was the best. Such a faith may seem strange to you, but maybe you will one day share it, if you will live. Esaias and I were so saddened when we first got the message of your father's death, and we could hardly believe it. Esaias first exclamation was: "Poor Knut! Please ask him to come to us to improve his own health!" (If you knew what an even and mild climate we have, and beautiful nature, you would come.)

Please relay to *your mother and sister* my greatest sympathy in the sorrow and loss that has befallen you all. All your family is precious to me. If it is not too painful, please tell me more details in your next letter. It would be interesting to know what he was last working on etc.

I have seen his name mentioned with great admiration in better American newspapers, but because of the lack of newspapers from home, I have lost track of the scientific developments in Sweden.

Out here we work so hard for our financial future, and even if we (like me) are still interested, we have no time to pay attention to everything. We lack books and magazines, or rather the funds to cover the large expense in getting them over here. American current literature is generally better and more genuine than the Swedish, but scientific magazines are lacking. Here we are mainly interested in discoveries that have a direct influence on our material progress. There is a general generosity towards science here, but since people are mainly focused on everyday survival, no great local scientists are nurtured. A child needs first of all food and clothing; this is true in America just as in other countries, although America is a giant in material resources.

Back to you. Otto Fries scared me when he mentioned something about your health. I hope there is nothing really serious. Don't let the recent sad event drive you into enforced studies that will jeopardize the best earthly gift we have—our health. If you only knew how happy I would be to see you here with me for a year or two. Thousands of persons with chest ailments and physical weakness get well here, every year. This is the Italy of America, but with milder winters and without the typhoons. We have such a mild climate and such clean fresh air in the pine forests and by the lakes. Once in a while, those who work hard outside in the midday sun fall ill with light fever, but for those who don't do physical work, the climate is very pleasant. I suppose I speak to deaf ears. But think about this invitation to stay with me in my new house. I will build the kitchen this month, and the main home in December or January, in the Swedish way.

I can send you all kinds of information about land and conditions, if you want. You mustn't think that I live in the wilderness. All the land around me is settled, mostly by educated, decent people. We have a post office, church, school and general store.

In the spring of 1877 I intend to visit Sweden (if I am alive and healthy) and could then accompany you on your journey back home.

Here you would have a rich field for botanical and zoological studies, so you wouldn't waste your time. I have horses, and we could make excursions. I have traveled a lot in Florida and am well acquainted with the land and people, which would be useful for you. If only I had time, myself, to study!

It seems like things are looking up for me financially.

My 161 acres are rapidly increasing in value. My health is good and so is my mental disposition. Yesterday I was offered a contract to plant 1000 wild orange trees for $1000. I will probably accept it as I can make $200 a month profit from it. I need to drive 70 miles to get the trees. Others have offered me cows and calves for orange trees. By being careful and prudent with acquiring, transporting and planting my current trees, I have had unusual success with them.

The prairies where I got lost last Christmas no longer frighten me. I now know roads and paths and can cross them in the pitch dark night if needed.

Jack, the pony I bought at Christmas escaped after two months. I had left him unfettered in the nearby forest. I found him in St. Augustine, 150 miles from here, emaciated and badly treated. Jack recognized me immediately, after three months separation, and now he is well on his way to getting fat and sturdy again! He is everybody's favorite—a strong and smart workhorse, as good as a mule and much nicer! I have bought Wilhelm's mule and wagon, and if I accept the orange tree contract I probably have to buy another one. These are expensive, $150 each. I am quitting the mill this month.

Now you know something about my outer economy. The inner one is also good. I know the language, laws and conditions so that I get along well and can take an interest in current events. Wherever I go I am treated with courtesy and hospitality. The Americans, even the poorest and simplest of them, behave nobly and are always polite. However, don't expect them to make big sacrifices—except in charities, where they surpass all other nations.

Tell me about your studies, relationships and summer adventures! Tell me about the sailing trips, the parties etc.

Your friend Josef

According to Knut's grandson, a rough time began for Knut after his father's death. He was given a despotic guardian, Professor Thalen, who caused Knut so much emotional distress that his health deteriorated even further.

In spite of his health problems, Knut finished high school in 1877, and began to study physics at the Upsala University.

Knut's and Josef's correspondence stopped for a few years.

Josef kept working on his farm in Florida. In 1877, he visited Sweden. (This was when he brought along an alligator which he let loose in the Göta canal...) He met Knut, but they didn't have much in common anymore. Knut was deeply involved in scientific studies and Josef had been away from science too long. He could not share Knut's interests, and Knut didn't ask much about Josef's life in Florida. The meeting was a disappointment for both of them.

Josef returned in January 1878, bringing with him a ten-year-old boy, Emil Almgren, (probably related to Robert Almgren who had worked with Josef in the past) apparently as a servant.

Although there are no more letters to Knut until 1880, I do have a letter from Josef to Salomon, from Lake Maitland, dated November 19, 1878. It gives some insight into Josef's current life. Here Josef responded to Salomon's suggestion that Josef should become a dentist if he stayed in Florida. Josef replied that such an education, in a college in Philadelphia, would take three years and cost $150. Room, board, clothes etc. would cost $250 a year. It was too expensive. Still, it was tempting, because it was getting too hard and hot to work in the summers in Florida.

Then Josef discussed politics and said that people are basically the same anywhere in the world. The same activities are always being repeated in various forms. In Sweden, things happened in a more covert way, keeping up the outer appearance of decency. Josef's eyes had been opened to this when he was young and his father Lars had told him about the intrigues in the Stockholm Parliament. Here in the U.S. things were done openly and were thus easier to discover and to oppose.

The Republicans currently had a difficult time, but Josef had succeeded in getting his congressman elected a couple of weeks earlier, on November 5. If the few Republicans who were still in power would be voted out, it would be political death for the Negroes. Josef had held a meeting with the Negroes, urging them to stick together and to support the party that had freed them from slavery and still cared about them. He explained to them about paper money and what happens if you print too much of it. He held a similar meeting with the Swedes, explaining to them too about gold, silver and paper money.

The elections this year had been calm in Florida, but fraudulent and violent in South Carolina, Louisiana and Mississippi. In one parish in Louisiana, thirty-seven Negroes had been fired at with a canon and had been killed. The current president of the U.S., Hayes, was superior to Grant in character and morals, but too hesitant to act when it was needed.

Josef had been quite ill with dysentery, called "bloody flux." He almost passed out the first day, and had to stay in bed for a week. Since Henrik Lilljebjörn, who normally lived with Josef, was working over at Sofia's lot that week, Josef was alone in his house. Luckily his neighbor Mr. Kedney was around, and checked on Josef every day.

One day when Josef was still very sick in bed, a black man came to visit. He made a tincture from the bark of a root that grew abundantly in the pine forest, and made Josef drink it. It helped, and within two days Josef was well enough to walk 5 miles to Sofia's house! Josef didn't know the name of the root, but described it; it looked similar to a beetroot and was hard, white and wooden inside. The bark, or shell, was softer. It was used for fever as well. Josef was going to send Salomon a sample of it. (He may have been talking about Wild Yam.)

In May 1879 Josef had completed his homestead years and could sell his land if he wanted. This year he also became a U.S. citizen.

In June of the same year, Knut got back in communication with Josef. Strangely enough, it took Josef half a year to reply to Knut's letter.

Letter 10 from Josef to Knut

Lake Maitland, Orange County, January 12, 1880
(*Knut's birthday*)

Dearest Knut,

You didn't receive a birthday letter from me this year, but I do remember the day, as you can see on the date above.

I got your letter from 4 June 1879, and it made me very happy because you told me a little about yourself. I suppose I can now congratulate you on your B.A. And I hope your health improved during the summer.

Last summer was boring here. I long for company and don't feel as happy here as I used to. My health is good but I can no longer work in the sun like I did in the past. I can handle the 30 or 35 degrees Celsius, but can no longer absorb the direct rays. Also I am a little fatter now than I was before the trip to Sweden. I weigh 191 pounds now in summer clothes. (*Josef was six feet tall.*) I always long for the cool winter weather, but this year it is very mild. So far we have only had one N.W. wind. Then the temperature fell to 0 Celsius just before sunrise, in a few places where the ground was wet and swampy. Not even bananas or pineapple froze, only part of the sweet potatoes (Convolvulus Batatas), but now they are green and blooming again.

We live between the temperate zone and the tropics. A few trees and bushes are now bare and will not get new leaves until February or March or even April. Others, like the oaks, shed their leaves when the new ones bud. But most trees are always green. And this winter they grow without interruption. The orange and lemon trees have new long shoots, and the pineapple is growing well. One is bearing fruit right now, half the size of a man's head. Most of the trees bear fruit in the autumn. Almost anything grows here, but you have to fertilize almost everything. This is not true for hammock land, only for pineland. In Sweden we are used to fertilizing, but in America it is unusual, and expensive, whether you buy guano or chemicals, or use swamp soil which you compost with potash or quicklime. The third method is to keep cows just for the manure. In the daytime they walk outside, and at night they are driven into a pen, which gradually is moved over the field. But that is risky, too. My previous neighbor, Schough, (he had another name in Sweden) bought three cows, took them home, and let them out to pasture the next day. He never saw them again. There are no pens or fences to stop them from walking to the Arctic Ocean or to Patagonia in the south.

If he had been smart and kept the calves at home, the cows would have returned home in the evening. That is the secret. It is more difficult with cows which have no calves, or with the steers. Those you have to search for miles, and if you have many, you will lose one or more every year. Someone else becomes the happy owner.

You have to search the forest frequently, early and late, come rain or shine, to keep your herd together. You also have to make sure you have good relations with your neighbors, so that they will give you truthful information on where the herd was last seen etc.

Sometimes they sink into the swamp, and one day you find the white bones, cleaned up by vultures, raccoons and possums.

But temporary losses are more than well compensated by the fact that the food for the cows doesn't cost anything. So far I haven't had any cattle, but I need to get twenty or twenty-five, as soon as I have the money. I have sold 20 acres of partly cleared but unplanted land of my homestead, but will not receive payment for a while.

I have now completed my duty of settling and cultivating my homestead land, of which every citizen can receive 160 acres. Tell me Knut, where else in the world can you find such a generous country? In America you are permitted to go out and choose your own land, and they give it to you for free, as long as you live there for five years, cultivate part of it and build a house, even if a very simple one. Millions of people have become rich just from this.

A railway will now be built from Sanford, our loading dock by the St. Johns River. It will run through Maitland and down to the west coast of Florida. By spring we will hear the whistle.

You can hardly find a better climate than here. At Christmas we had + 25 Celsius at midday, and in the mornings +15 to +20 in a non-heated room. The wind has been mostly the usual southeastern trade wind, but slightly more east. Rain only about once a month, but we got plenty of water in the late summer and autumn.

So you are not in love yet? Well, neither am I, and what is worse, I don't think I ever will be. Soon I will be too old for it. But if I will continue to live this way, it would be wiser to get married, in love or not. I had almost forgotten my promise to you. Wasn't it that *you* were to find a bride for me? I still hold you to this!

The girls you used to refer to as my sweethearts are always taken. Julia is married in Portland, Maine, and has three children. Lydia is a well-to-do lady living in a street not far from you, and little Albertina, the prettiest of them, has passed away. So now you have to pick a woman for me and send her as first class cargo, paid on arrival! She needs to bring some money, unless she wants to cook our food herself. Here a cook gets $15 a month plus all expenses paid.

You need a rich wife if you are going to pay the cook 672 Swedish kronor a year and the maid 400-500 kronor. It pays better to be a maid than a wife. However, if you find a suitable girl for me, send her over. Better send a photo first, just in case. The return shipping is expensive. But if you swear to me that you would want her yourself, then I will take her uninspected.

My political friends have proposed me as postmaster in Maitland. I have made no attempt whatsoever to obtain this job, and therefore will not grieve if I don't get it. The great gentlemen in Washington can do as they please. I would receive 60% of all postage that is stamped here, plus rent for the mailboxes from people who wish to have their own P.O. boxes. Some people say the income will be $100-200, some say $200-300. The former is more likely. It hardly pays off to maintain the place yourself unless you also have a general store or some other subsidiary income.

And now I want to say a few words about our politics, which you don't seem to understand or like. Since not every citizen exercises his right to vote at the elections, a governing body is often not an expression of the wish of the people. Instead it represents a clique, or even worse, a group of demagogues. But if you have an opinion, and consider one of the parties to be harmful, if is of course correct to try to get others to vote the way *you* do. The representatives and politics of the parties are thoroughly scrutinized at election times, and that can only be healthy. Even if it is unfair and mixed with slander. Tricks and bribes are best prevented by publicity, and even if false stories are often spread, it is still better than putting a muzzle on the press. Politics in America currently has two big tasks to solve. First, to consolidate the results of the civil war, the freedom and equality of the Negroes and all citizens, and second, the solution of the economic questions.

The Democrats here in the South, although they pretend to accept the 14th and 15th Amendments to the Constitution, are actually trying to oppress the Negroes and remove their right to vote. With tricks or violence they hinder them from exercising their right to vote. Also by not giving them equal rights to schools and education, and by making laws in the southern states that are beneficial only to the plantation owners. Republican parties are doing the opposite.

When it comes to economy, the Democrats praise paper money and try to pay governmental debts in coins that are worth less than had been promised. The Republicans are honest, use gold and silver coins and therefore pay fully. I cannot neglect to have opinions regarding all these things, and to *state* my opinions and *work* for them. I also need a little jolt out of my normal daily life.

Best regards to your mother, sister and brother-in-law, and don't forget your old friend Josef

Letter 11 from Josef to Knut

Altamonte, January 11, 1881

Dearest Knut,

Happy New Year to you—when you start a new one tomorrow on your birthday. I want to thank you for two letters. I am not at all offended by what you write. What you say is true and right, that a human being should occupy himself with one endeavor, and not split himself up on many things, if he wants to get somewhere in this world.

But what if a person doesn't have goals to make major contributions in science or art? What if he just wants to quietly pursue his happiness in a way he sees fit?

Among the duties we have in life, the foremost one is towards ourselves. When we have our final accounts with the Lord, the first thing we need to show is our own inner development. He will not ask us what we have accomplished, but how we have behaved. I don't know if I would have been a better or wiser man if I had become a practicing physician or a school teacher. The knocks and set-backs you experience in the varied and multi-faceted life in this free country educate you just as good, and maybe better, than the narrow, straight habits in Sweden. For those who keep their eyes and ears open, and are able to draw conclusions, life out here is a good school. At least it has been so for me.

My *nearest* goal here has been and is to become financially independent. I am glad to say that it moves in the right direction. Times are good and the properties, in which I have my wealth, are rising in value. Last winter I sold a piece of land for $1100, which gave me some space to breathe. I estimate the value of my properties to $10,000, if I sell them sensibly. I buy and sell land for myself, and have considered doing it for others as well, with commissions.

At Christmas we had a bit of cold weather with a wind from the north. The pineapples are still outside, uncovered, but when there is a threat of frost I cover them with fabric. I have covered 2800 seedlings with palm leaves, to protect them from possible frost this month. This is the time to plant orange trees. Last Saturday I planted forty-five Mandarin orange trees—they are dwarf trees, with small, highly valued oranges.

Sunday I did something I have never done before— christened three toddlers! For two years I had refused, but since no Lutheran priest has come to us, I finally accepted. One girl, Viola Christina, two and a half years old, almost made me laugh. She smiled so mischievously when I poured water over her. First we read from the Bible, which we often do, and then we had the christening. Now that the ice is broken I suppose I will have to do this often, because another child is expected, and ten babies a year is not unusual among the Swedes here.

In politics things have calmed down again. In the last campaign I was the secretary of Orange County Republican Executive Committee, but I didn't participate as much in the feuds as I did four years ago, when I almost got shot in Jesup by some fanatic Democrats.

As you know I have been lucky regarding accidents. But last summer my horse bolted, when I was transporting some fine pedigree pigs in a carriage, from Sanford to my place here. The reins got snared around my fingers and pulled so hard that the bone in my right index finger broke, and blood came out under my nail. Afterwards I almost fainted from pain and exhaustion. Now it's OK, but the finger is somewhat stiff.

I still live in a simple lumber house with bare walls only decorated by a few portraits, yours among them. I could afford to build something better, but since I don't know if I will stay here, this has to suffice for now. Perhaps I will go somewhere else. It is better to put the money into things that rise in value. Houses just rot, and there are so many other beneficial ways to invest ones money. For example, a good mortgage yields 10 -18% interest or even higher.

I am happy to say that Otto Fries has become a decent and orderly man. (*Apparently Otto had been misbehaving or drinking.*) I haven't visited them for a year, but will soon go. There is not much entertainment here other than fresh air and a mild climate. You live for your business; you talk and even dream about it.

A bear and a few lynxes have attacked the poultry houses in our area this winter, but luckily they have been shot. The gray fox is still a threat to ducks and chicken, and the hawk threatens my grapes. Wild ducks swim in the pond outside our house, but I don't have time to bother them.

Ask Thore Fries if he received a package of Epidendrum Venosum, a beautiful air plant, by mail for the Botanical Garden.

Please give my best regards to your mother, sister and brother-in-law

Your old friend Josef

In 1880 Knut sent a couple of letters to Josef, but Josef did not reply. The next year, 1881, Knut published his first paper at the Swedish Royal Academy of Science— "The volume change of water through the absorption of gases". He sent a copy to Josef.

Letter 12 from Josef to Knut

Altamonte, March 19, 1882

My dear beloved boy!

It was a sad and surprising letter I received from you yesterday. You are ill and depressed and you even doubt our friendship. I understand that you feel that way, because this is the second or third letter I have received from you, as well as your scientific paper, that I have not replied to. But I certainly have not forgotten you. You are frequently in my thoughts and your portrait is one of the few that hang in my room. I have sat down twice to start a letter to you, on my birthday December 22 and on yours January 12, but have been interrupted. I didn't think my letters were good enough to send. Especially since I usually write spontaneously, seldom read what I have written, and then send it off.

But you cannot seriously believe that I no longer feel warmly about you. It is true that I have become calmer, and no longer express my feelings of joy or sorrow or other passions, like I used to. But even if I don't express them, our friendship is as deep as ever.

I liked you so much, and had so much pleasure in seeing you when you were a child. I had to force myself to spend less time with you, when we met in the English Park or in your house or mine. Sometimes I tried to not see you for two or three weeks.

When I went to America, I didn't say goodbye to you, because it would have increased the sorrow of parting. I hoped that when you grew up we would become true friends and confidants. When I came back after six years absence, you were an adult, involved in your studies and concentrating on your goals. For myself, I had been gone too long from scientific studies. My direct interest in them, especially in their details, had cooled down. Six years of practical work here, under conditions so different from those in Sweden, had considerably changed my view on life. My opinions on what really matters in life, and what earthly joy consists of, had changed.

Also, I was dejected and worried about some of my business ventures, and that made me less inclined to recreate our old friendship and see you as often as I otherwise would have. It was the same with the few other friends I still had in Upsala—they all complained about my passivity.

But if you would ever need help, if there would be a practical way to prove my friendship, you would find me unchanged.

Your earlier silence also made me believe that my sloppy letters did not interest you. And since my inclination for letter writing is irregular, and I was more and more occupied with my business (more than I should, it often keeps me awake at night when I try to sleep) I postponed writing to you so that my letter would arrive on your birthday. One evening I started a letter to you, but the next morning I had to go to southern Apopka, where I am starting a 25-acre orange and lemon orchard, and then I never finished the letter. But I hope I will get better at writing.

I feel great compassion for your physical suffering, your sadness caused by that, and the interruption of your studies. I rejoice in the successes of my friends. It is great when some people succeed in the world, and even better when they are my friends. I can understand that you are bored when you are not working, while your poor body is recuperating. But you should not be melancholic. So far you have used your time well and fairly successfully. Many people lose a few years some way or another, and that is all right.

Life is short, but success comes slowly for most people. Unless you are pressured by financial problems, which I hope is not the case, it doesn't matter if you complete your education a year earlier or later. I am sure, that when you have become a teacher, professor or engineer or whatever you are hoping for, you will find it of minor importance that it happened a year earlier or later. It is of small importance compared to caring for your physical health, without which there surely is very little earthly pleasure.

Therefore the time is not wasted when you care for your health. Perhaps you think I am talking nonsense. Maybe I am, but I am talking from my own experiences of illness. I would rather be a simple day worker in good health all my life, than a high civil servant or rich capitalist with a sick body and grumpy disposition.

When I was young I often dreamed about fast success and happiness, which never materialized. Nothing succeeded for me until I learned to be patient and accept things as they are and make the best out of all existing situations.

Oh, how hard it was sometimes to see my hopes and dreams shatter. Patience, patience, patience infinitely! Start over or take another route. Life is actually a continuous battle against small, insignificant events which still are of great importance if you neglect them. They are all linked together. I would almost believe the Muslim doctrine about a blind destiny, if I did not also observe that one's direct actions constantly modify the effects of fate.

This is no comfort for you, and not meant as such. I just want you to see that other people also have had times of sorrow, and can sympathize with you. But better days will come. If you would feel that a winter in the mild Florida climate would do you good, then remember that it would be a great pleasure for me to have you here. My only concern is how you would feel without the care from your mother, which you have never so far been without. The comforts are not great here, and I have no library, but the change of environment might make it bearable for you in the winter and possibly for a year. Many people, with illness similar to yours, have regained health and appetite by just being in this climate and doing some light chores in the fresh air.

In any case, I hope you make it your main goal to regain your health.

I wish my economic situation was such that I could send you a ticket. Although I have a fair amount of land, it unfortunately is still non-productive, so I don't have the money. I am hoping that everything will progress as it should, so that I no longer have to deny myself the pleasure of seeing my friends.

This winter has been pleasant, and now it will soon be warm again. We already have +36 Celsius in the shade at midday. However, a nice breeze cools us, and our clothing is of course light—only a wool shirt and pants and straw hat.

There have been a lot of tourists and speculators here, but my little patch in the forest is 5 miles from railroad and hotels, so I don't see much of them.

In January I got two workers, a boy and a girl from Sweden. Since then it has been livelier and nicer in my home. Now you, if you visit me, don't have to worry about doing your own cooking and dishwashing. Although only seventeen, the girl is quite capable. She has breakfast ready at sunrise 6:00 a.m., and keeps the rooms orderly. My previous cook, Emil, who used

to be a small sickly boy, constantly suffering from inflammation of nose, ears and chest, has become a healthy and strong young man. He was glad to get out of the kitchen and ... will continue soon.
(Letter ends abruptly in mid sentence.)

By 1883 Josef had begun to do well financially. It was now he who took on indentured servants from Sweden...

In one contract, from January 1883 (owned by Joseph Raymond and donated to the Sanford Museum) Josef agreed to pay the passage from Upsala to Orange County for a K.W. Andersson. The cost was 200 Swedish kronor. The boy would be an agricultural laborer with no salary for one year. The work had to be done cheerfully and with care—this was part of the contract! He would do all the work Josef could reasonably ask him to perform. He would carefully handle Josef tools, treat Josef's animals and cattle well, and be satisfied with his food and accommodations.

Josef promised to treat the boy fairly, take care of him in case of illness, and give him enough food. After one year Josef would give him 5 acres of land suitable for growing oranges. Esaias, who had been back in Sweden for several years, acted as Josef's attorney and was one of the signatories on the contract.

Josef also took on an eleven-year-old boy, the boy's father signing the contract.

In August Josef made a 16-month contract with Maria Josefina Andersson from Upsala to be a servant for him. He gave her a third-class passage to America, including all expenses. He would lodge and feed her, and help her if she was ill. She would get one dollar a month to buy her own clothes. The work would consist of cooking, washing, mending and housekeeping. She too had to promise to do all the work that he could reasonably ask of her—cheerfully and with care! She was to obey all reasonable orders.

In October, Josef's neighbor Mr. Kedney also got a Swedish servant, Johanna Strömberg. Esaias was again the attorney-in-fact. Johanna would get no salary for 13 months, and was to make herself generally useful. (Later Johanna married Josef's cousin Rudolf Henschen.)

December 10, 1883 Josef wrote to his father:
"Dear beloved Father! It was a great joy to receive your letter and to hear about your health and conditions at home. I hope you will keep your good health and good spirits for many more years. I hope I will once again be able to see you and hug you and thank you for all the love you have given me. Thank you also for your financial help, without which I would not have succeeded here as well as I have. In this new year I hope you will keep experiencing the inner joy and harmony which is the most important thing in life."

Lars had again asked Josef to return to Sweden, and to find a wife, but Josef vehemently disagreed. Josef said he could not create any interest in Swedish politics and conditions—he had developed new interests and opinions in America.

Sofia had recently died, at age seventy-eight. Josef discussed some practical details regarding her estate. There were no other letters about Sofia's death, so it is presumed that a cable was sent at the time.

In late 1883, Knut was very ill and wrote a sad letter to Josef.

Letter 13 from Josef to Knut

Altamonte, December 23, 1883

My dearest Knut!
You probably believe that our old friendship is over and finished since I never write to you. Part two of my

last letter was never completed. I have become sluggish and neglectful in all letter writing except business correspondence. It would not be surprising if my friends believe that Mammon has completely occupied my heart. But this is not the case. In situations where I am able to help, I am always willing and ready. But facing your melancholia, caused by your illness, I felt truly helpless. It makes me very sad. I was hoping that you would soon get better. I would like to know how you are doing now.

I have sometimes suggested that this climate, and some light physical work here for a period, would do you good. You would be warmly welcomed.

My financial situation has improved from year to year, through property speculation and frugal living. You must not believe that you would be an economic burden for me. As you know, you would be a dear guest and good company for me.

When your letter arrived, Miss Sjöborg was still alive. She was full of sympathy for your condition and immediately suggested that I invite you to come here. But right then I had a full house and was not sure of my plans. Our old friend Rulle, Rudolf Henschen, was staying with me. He had not been able to resist the temptations of the cheerful camaraderie in Sweden, and also had some adversities, plus a basically melancholic nature. He started drinking, damaging his future and his health. But now he is a changed man, hard working, well behaved and beginning to stand on his own feet. I have also had another young relative here, helping him out. He is gone now. I would have much preferred to have your dear face here, in real life, not just on the picture that always hangs on my wall.

I am sorry I haven't written to you. But you have often been in my thoughts, and I have celebrated your birthday and other holidays by remembering you. Thank you again for the first edition of your scientific paper. If you cannot continue your studies, because of your health, remember that we can reach our goals in this world in more ways than one. Even if it feels bitter to see hopes and plans go to pieces. I tell you this out of experience, because my plans were very different from the life I now live, and I have many times felt that life was not worth living. Perhaps it was my own fault, which is not the case with you. But in the long run, you may see that your situation will become useful for you, as I am beginning to think mine has for me. We cannot see our future and what will later be of use for us.

My only hesitation is whether you would be bored here, since you would hardly be interested in our activities. Also you are very fragile. Maybe you need special food which we don't have here. Tell me how you are doing, and the details of your illness and diet.

My life here is somewhat monotonous, but for a year or two it may offer you the delights of a new environment. You would have plenty of opportunity to study botany and ornithology, and we have an abundance of insects. The only entomologists we have here are chickens and quails.

If business should interest you, there is plenty of opportunity for small as well as large speculations. A safe and good way to double a small capital is to start an orange orchard.

You can buy, plant and nurse 1000 trees, all expenses included, for $500. After a year they are worth $1000. If you add another $400-500 for work, fertilizing and maintenance, they would be worth $2000-2500 the next year. The third year, with the same expenses, they will be worth $3000-5000. This is the current price. You only need about two acres for such an operation. There is an incredible amount of opportunities here to make money. But perhaps this doesn't interest you. Perhaps you are only interested in abstract things. But maybe it would please you to be here and make some income, and go home with a bit of money.

Here I sit, planning and fantasizing for you, while you probably have no interest or possibility to come. But you are welcome if you feel like it. There is no socializing or entertainment here. I am talking about the sort of entertainment you have at home—concerts, theatre, parties, grand openings of homes and parks, etc. I don't associate with anyone, except for business meetings, but that can sometimes be several times a week.

It is a true pleasure for me to sit peacefully on my veranda, surrounded by roses, oleander, blooming jasmine and hibiscus protecting me from the sun.

For Christmas I have been invited to Mrs. Sellmer, who took a liking to me after 15 minutes conversation. (I have more luck with married ladies than with single girls, though I admit I have never tried to befriend the latter.) Her husband is a lieutenant in the army (was a colonel in the civil war) and is coming home for Christmas. He is in some fort far away in the west, fighting the Indians. She lives in Florida and has built and maintained an orange plantation so that they can become financially independent and he can leave the army. Ah, this is the American Woman! They have a lovely daughter with golden locks and sky-blue eyes. She won my heart right away with her smile, and I had better stay away from her. Too bad that she is only twelve and I turned forty yesterday. You have to pity me, Knut. I am now in my forties approaching my fifties and have not yet found a life companion. I have gray temples. Perhaps it is the damn money that has turned my hair gray. Probably not. I could have had a better time out here if I had known what I know now, but hindsight is always easy. However, it may be useful for my friends.

I now have five permanent workers, and two boys and a girl, a sister to the boys, who cooks. And I have two extra workers doing piece work. It is not always pleasant in the house. You need to be patient and smart to handle the workers and keep them in good spirits and well behaved. Most of all, you need patience and tolerance. In about a year I will probably shrink the household.

I wish you a Happy Birthday, and send you my card on a piece of skin from a rattlesnake. I caught him alive, kept him in a cage for five months, but he resisted all influence of civilization and fasted until he died. He was 6 feet long, 11 rattles.

Best wishes to your mother, sister, brother-in-law and yourself—I will always be your old friend Josef.

By 1884, Knut's health was much better. He received his Master's Degree in Physics, traveled in Europe, and visited the German physicist August Kundt who had a new laboratory in Strasbourg on the French-German border. He sent a letter to Josef.

Letter 14 from Josef to Knut

Lake Maitland, April 27, 1884

My best friend Knut!

I seldom feel like replying to letters from friends and family, because my attention is too much fixated on business, speculations and small problems. If I forget to keep my goal, financial independence, always before my eyes, I can easily become irritated and preoccupied. I have to travel a lot on dusty roads, I come home tired, find that the boys or workers have been lazy or behaved badly or failed to do their work, and wagons or horses have been damaged. In such circumstances I don't feel like sitting down to write letters as they might convey tiredness or bad moods.

This is why your dear letter has not yet been answered. But today, Sunday, feeling lazy and somewhat bothered by the heat (+ 31 C in the shade) I opened the Daily Paper from Stockholm. There I was happily surprised to see that you have received your Masters Degree. That gave me another reason to write to you and warmly congratulate you. I am sure your mother hugged you when you came home. She was probably even happier than you. I imagine myself in your circle of friends, giving you a warm hug.

It is now twenty-one years ago that we first met and became friends. I have changed a lot, and the many years in this boisterous country have changed my view on life, my interests and opinions about people and conditions. I have become harder and more closed up, as a result of disappointments in myself and other people, but my mind is still open to the joy and success of others. Especially those of my friends. You are one of the foremost in old Sweden, even when I count my relatives.

Your letter made me happy on several accounts, mainly because you so suddenly have regained your health! The anguished cry in your earlier letter touched me so deeply. I felt so helpless, having to be a Job's consoler and always telling you to be patient. It is so much better to now be able to rejoice with you. I was also glad to see that during your illness you have directed your gaze both inwards and outwards to conditions in life that have not previously interested you. When earlier you wrote that I should discard politics and instead work towards a goal, I understood that your interest in the various events of society and people's future had not yet been awakened.

If you want something practical done, and to see some reforms take place in your lifetime, then it is not enough to talk and write about your convictions. You actually have to put your hand into the political machinery at the elections. I have found that you can get a lot done in an honest and legal way, and can avoid dirty intrigues and deceptions.

Political hatred is rampant here since the civil war, and has often caused bloodshed, murder and persecution. You cannot avoid that your opponents hate you, but if you voice your opinions in a firm, unafraid and honest way, you will find even here that you become more respected than the silent people. Cowardly passivity is common here, even among our Swedish countrymen.

However, I have in an unnoticed and non-calculated way come to take your advice more and more. My interest in politics has decreased in the same rate that my business has increased and been successful. Also, the political questions have been solved, and the conditions that were created by the civil war have been more and more consolidated. But the laws regarding equality of the Negroes in the elections are still thwarted in several southern states, by the previous slave party, or rather by the young people who have grown up in these traditions. They threaten and trick the Negroes at the elections. Apart from that there is hardly any difference between the parties anymore. It is mainly about who will have the power and the offices.

New questions, or actually old forgotten ones are now coming up again, like free trade and protective customs, reform of the ways to elect officials, coins, the question of gold or silver or both. And the rights of the big corporations versus the states and individuals. In the future we will see, here as in Europe, an enormous battle between workers and capitalists. These questions will modify or break up the current parties. I hope it will be soon, because lacking major problems, the corruption and lust for power become the main occupation.

However, you should not believe all the exaggerated and ridiculous stories about corruption that you hear about. The unlimited freedom of the press is being ruthlessly abused by political opponents, especially at election times, and 50% of their stories are false. And just as often they are complete lies.

At the last elections I was fairly calm, and I feel no need to be active this autumn. Maybe I have become too comfortable and selfish, but my enthusiasm for politics has all but expired.

The big questions that agitate you in Sweden have been solved here a hundred years ago by the Declaration of Independence. Although the fate and battles of my old native country still interest me very much, I can only smile about the current clamor and trivialities there. Frightened priests who will not allow different sects to meet and discuss their mutual goals. They resist the Evangelical Alliance, naively unaware that their own church is just a sect, and a somewhat withered one, among the Christian religions. New parties are being cultivated for their own selfish goals. The Enforced Oath is sending conscientious people to jail, those very people who without the oath would speak the truth.

Here, people are allowed to swear or solemnly declare what they choose. Punishment for crimes is the same for everyone. Yes, the Chinese is allowed to slaughter his rooster and swear by its blood. It is only a question of time until the King will be considered redundant both in Norway and Sweden. He cannot change the times and events, but keeps making pompous speeches.

But, let the dead bury the dead and let me answer your letter. You ask if I have rolled oats. I should think so! We used to eat them three times a day, but I try to limit it to twice a day. I can get butter from the store, but not always the freshest, as they buy it from New York. Sometimes we have fresh meat, but sometimes the butcher doesn't come, or is gone for a while. I can always offer you canned meat, if you want to visit. You can't get milk where I live now, but I have condensed, canned milk. I don't think the food will be a problem generally. But summer is not a suitable time to visit. The heat makes you inactive. Expeditions or longer trips become unpleasant or even bad for your health, because of rain and mosquitoes. But winter and spring, from November to May, are usually the nicest you can imagine, and even people with weak constitutions will thrive in the forest and countryside.

My home is very simple. Because of my good health I have neglected to protect my house from the cold wind and light frost that often occur in December and January. But that could be easily corrected if you should decide to come here. However, I think we should use the time to do some traveling. We could make a trip to Central America, via New Orleans and its World Exhibition. I would love to finally see the tropics, together with a scientist like you. We could measure some mountain tops and look down into some volcanoes and make various scientific observations. I would bring a bunch of plants back to Florida, and I would take a look at some coffee plantations, to see if they could be more lucrative than oranges here. It would also be all right if we happened to find a gold mine or silver mine among the mountains. You would become the chief engineer and I the director, and both of us owners. And if I would also find a dark-eyed Spanish girl who would enchant me, the trip would be perfect. I have always admired dark-eyed girls but have never found a face as beautiful as the eyes. Perhaps in the end I will settle for a pair of blue.

This reminds me of your promise to find a girl for me. If I keep up my current life style for another ten years I will certainly remain single. Apart from my business acquaintances I have no social life and don't strive to get it. Usually I decline the invitations I get. Business fills my mind much too much. The only way to change it would be to leave this area for a while.

One business transaction creates the next and I am always thinking of new opportunities. Sometimes they keep me awake at night. But sometimes I sleep 10-12 hours and am lazy and relaxed. Yesterday I was up with the sun and went to Orlando with a Swedish lady, Mrs. Thollander. I helped her buy a piece of land, and ran around like a crazy person between land agents, owners and creditors. I found an auction in a storage house and bought, by old habit, a few unnecessary items, cheaply. Then I returned home in the dark of night with a bolting horse (my own "Darling") but without adventures, except that some small animal scared the horse so he almost toppled over.

This (Sunday) morning I got up at 8:00 a.m. and had breakfast—oatmeal and fried pork, cocoa with wheat bread and cheese. Then I walked in the orchard, swam in the cold pool, leafed through the newspapers. Had lunch at 1:30 p.m.—wild portulaca in white sauce, pickled salmon, fruit soup and some sweet delicious dessert. After that I tried in vain to read or take a nap. I received visitors and asked them to entertain themselves and leave me alone on the sofa. Towards the evening I chirped up, and after dinner (fresh fish with the rest of the portulaca) I first made sure that my "Darling" was well taken care of—I found she had been left without water and she welcomed me with a neigh. Then I got out my pen and paper to write this letter to you. Now you have an idea of what our Sundays are like. Oh yes, and we also had afternoon coffee and cake with the visitors.

Tomorrow I will be out running around again.

My financial problem right now is to transform part of my non-profitable land property—wild land in various places—into cash. I want to buy city property that I can rent out or build on, so that I get a regular income, which I completely lack at the moment. I bought seventeen city lots and two small homes in Orlando, for myself, just over a month ago. I am only paying $2150. Now the seller wants to buy it back, and give me another $1000, but I think I can double the purchase price by the winter, by selling the smaller lots and dividing the larger ones. I also want to keep some land to build on.

I have probably sold a 10-acre land lot with 300 small orange trees by Maitland, to a Scotsman, for $3000. Everything is agreed on except the funds.

Two months ago I sold 120 acres near the Atlantic coast for $1800. I had bought them for $200 a year ago.

I have also bought 120 acres of meadows and swamp for $350, and a few city lots in Maitland. And I am in the process of building and planting at my Apopka land 20 miles from here. So you see that I am keeping busy. My new home is beautiful, dark green, 1100 trees of all types. The fertilizing per year costs $200.

I still live in the same place but the post office and address has changed.

Please greet your mother respectfully from me, and write to your friend Josef

The same year, 1884, Knut got engaged to Helene Pilo, granddaughter of the prominent mathematician and astronomer Jöns Svanberg. Two years later Knut and Helene were married. There is a letter from Knut to his fiancée, dated June 7, 1884, about his friend Josef. Since all Knut's letters to Josef were destroyed in a fire, this is the only existing text that shows how Knut feels about Josef.

Knut's letter to Helene, about Josef

[...] this friendship has persisted with touching tenacity. I was a six-year-old child, when we first met, and he was then a young student. His interests were too large or rather too dispersed, and he lacked the ability to concentrate them. In spite of his bright intellect he did not take his exams, and then he went to America. It looked as though his old weakness would ruin him. He was pulled into politics, acted as an organizer for the Negroes, made political enemies who even tried to kill him, and had a hard time. He now owns a large orange orchard, deals in land and properties and is doing big business. He has sacrificed a lot for money, sacrificed various interests for this goal, sacrificed the old native country, and also sacrificed a home life.

Throughout all this rough time, he has preserved a warm friendship for the boy from whom he separated fourteen years ago. With great interest he participates in this boy's sorrows and joys, adversities and successes. The fact that his letters have never been rewarded with responses of proportionate length, and sometimes not been answered at all, makes his loyalty even more beautiful, in several ways.

It is a year and a half since I wrote to say good bye to him. (*Knut had thought he was going to die.*) Perhaps you know that I was very ill at that time. It took a while before his answer arrived—it is often difficult to reply to such letters. He asked me to come to Florida, as the good climate would be beneficial for my health. By that time I no longer needed the help he had offered, but that does not lessen my gratitude, and I know he is truly happy that I am now better. Now he is writing in a friendly and encouraging way about my exams, which he reads about in the paper. He rejoices with me and my mother, wishes that I would still come and visit for a while, and of course cannot restrain himself from ending his long letters with speculations about land, oranges, pounds etc. Of all the letters of congratulations I have received, only one has delighted and touched me more. (*Knut is referring to Helene's letter.*) So, now I have had the pleasure of presenting my oldest friend to you—with the exception of my father and mother. [...]

Josef was now forty-one years old, and his father and siblings in Sweden desperately wanted him to get married. They kept hinting about it in their letters, and sometimes told him outright to come back to Sweden so they could introduce him to some suitable women. Josef hated the idea, and usually ignored their suggestions.

In September Josef wrote to his father, with badly concealed resentment, that if he were to find a wife, it would have to happen spontaneously. A marriage had to be based on mutual affection and could not be arranged or enforced. He would like to make his father happy by finding a spouse, but would definitely not go to Sweden to find one! If he should feel like getting married, there were plenty of girls to choose from in Florida!

Nevertheless, Josef wrote to Lydia Bring in Sweden, more or less proposing to her. Lydia was a girl he had liked many years earlier, when he was a student in Upsala. She had married another man, who was much older than she. Josef began his letter: "Since your husband is probably dead by now [...]

The husband was definitely old, but far from dead, and was furious about the letter!

Lars Wilhelm Henschen, Josef's father, did not live to see Josef get married. He died January 27, 1885, at age eighty.

On February 22, 1885, Josef wrote to Salomon about their father:

"What a loving heart he had and what a loyal friend he was to all of us. He was old, and wanted to let go of his ailments, so I am not grieving. But it still feels empty and bitter to not one more time be able to hug him and see his dear face."

In the June 1885 Census of Orange County there was a Carolina Svensson listed as a servant living in Josef's household. She was a Swedish girl from the town of Karlskrona in Blekinge County, where Henschens had lived for generations. Carolina and her friend Inga (Persson) Larsson had arrived in New York on the SS Furnessia, on November 20, 1884. A couple of weeks later they were in Mellonville. We know very little about Carolina and how she ended up in Josef's home. Did he send for her? Did his Swedish relatives send her to him? The family legend has it that Josef sent for a "mail order bride", but there is no proof of this. She had a brother, Per Svensson, who lived in Chicago, but she went to Florida.

100

Carolina was born October 30, 1864, making her twenty-one years younger than Josef. She spoke no English.

Carolina and Josef were married December 8, 1885.

Josef did not mention the marriage to his family in Sweden until April 1, 1886, in a letter to my great-grandfather Salomon! He wrote, in passing, that he had been married for "quite a while"! That was all he said. He was probably embarrassed because Carolina was not the kind of high society girl his family would have wanted. Also, there was the fact that Carolina was pregnant when they wed—we know this because their first child was born in May 1886.

After the one line about the new wife, Josef changed the subject and wrote about business and every day life as usual. He ended the letter by telling Salomon that although he was fond of all his siblings, he loved Salomon and his wife Gerda the most.

The same year, 1885, Josef was approached by a man named Peter A. Demens. In The Swedish Pioneer Historical Quarterly *(July 1968), Ivar F. Pearson describes Demens as "the successful operator of a lumber business in Longwood, some 10 miles from Sanford. Demens was a Russian of noble ancestry, a political exile who had come to America to escape the tyranny of the Czarist regime. The Russian form of his name was Piotr Alexewich Dementieff which after arriving in this country, he changed to Peter A. Demens. A man of remarkable business talent and a born promoter [...]"*

Christine Best relates that Demens owned a small logging railroad that circled around the town of Longwood. He had named it the Orange Belt Railway. In 1885 he extended it to the town of Lake Monroe (which is now within Sanford city limits). From there Demens decided to take it west, to Oakland by Lake Apopka. He began looking for investors, and contacted Josef, as well as Henry Sweetapple, an Englishman, and A.M. Taylor, an American.

Historian Karl H. Grismer, in Tourist News, *February 16, 1924, quotes Josef: [...] "I was solicited by Andrew Johnson, a lawyer in Orlando, to join Peter A. Demens and A.M. Taylor in building a narrow-gauge railroad which they had started to build westward from Lake Monroe on the St. Johns River. Three miles of the road had been built with 16-pound rails Demens had bought from the South Florida Railroad, for his old log road running from the timberlands to his saw mills at Longwood. The road looked anything but good, but the men were full of hope and enterprise. However, their cash was spent and their stock of goods in the mill store was nearly gone."*

"I decided to join Demens and Taylor and wired them my decision to invest $10,000 and maybe more later."

"I was received with open arms as the savior of the railroad. Without my money the grading of the railroad would have been stopped and the project probably abandoned. Shortly afterwards I inherited some money from my father's estate, which enabled me to invest another $10,000 in the railroad enterprise. Later I turned over 1,000 acres of land to the company. To save money for the railroad, I took personal charge of the grading from Forest City. The road was completed from Lake Monroe to Oakland early in November, and on November 15, 1886, a free excursion was held to the new town, the settlers giving a free barbeque dinner. Hundreds attended."

Here is a quote from an article in the South Florida Argus, *November 18, 1886:*

"The people at Sylvan Lake (one of the stations on the road) had decorated the building (the depot) with palmetto, evergreens, bunting and flags, and from one of the three evergreen arches across the track there waved the flags of four nations; the Russian for Mr. Demens, the Swedish for Mr. Henschen, the English for Mr. Sweetapple and the American for Mr. Taylor, the four energetic, enterprising and public-spirited directors and builders of the road."

Office of P. A. DEMENS,

ARCHITECT AND CONTRACTOR.

Doors, Sash, Blinds,
Nails and Builders' Hardware,
Rough & Dressed-Lumber,
Mouldings, Brackets, Balusters, Newel Posts, &c.
Building Materials of all Kinds.

Plans and Specifications made; Estimates
on them furnished, and Architectural Work and
Contracting done in all branches.

Sole Agent for South Florida for Asbestos Materials.

Longwood, Fla., Apr. 1st 1886

Käreste Broder Salomon!

Jag sände dig för en två veckor sedan 1847 genom Ankarlinien att utbetalas till dig genom Capt. Leonard Borg och förvandlas i kronor efter bästa kurs i Newyork. Hade jag vetat att vexel i dollars varit fördelaktigare såsom Wilhelm nu skrifver så hade jag låtit acceptera

Letter from Josef to his brother Salomon April 1ˢᵗ, 1886. (Courtesy of Uppsala University Library.)

Orange Belt Railway train. (Courtesy of the Museum of Seminole County History.)

On January 6, 1887, there was another article about the railroad in the Argus. The following was said about Josef: "Mr. Henschen, who is the company's representative here, is progressive in his ideas and is pushing the work of improvement on as fast as possible."

According to Ivar Pearson, Demens wanted Josef not only for his money, but for his spirit of enthusiasm which was contagious.

When the railroad had reached Oakland, Josef was satisfied. The Orange Belt headquarters were now in this town, and many new shops and other buildings, as well as a large hotel, were quickly constructed. A canal from Lake Apopka to Lake Dora, connecting it to the St. Johns River, Sanford and Jacksonville was also completed. In 1887 Josef and Carolina moved to Oakland and built their home there. Oakland boomed and Demens became its first mayor.

Orange Belt Railway Depot, Oakland. (Courtesy of the Museum of Seminole County History.)

Then Demens decided to extend the railroad to Pinellas Point on the Florida west coast. Josef thought this was a crazy idea, since there was already a railroad from Sanford to Tampa, the South Florida Railroad, owned by Henry B. Plant. But Josef was outvoted by the others, and forced to go along with the plans. They borrowed $900,000 from Armour, Drexel, and E.W. Clark in Philadelphia.

Grismer quotes Josef saying: "An Italian padrone was sent down to start grading although the surveys across the sand hills were not even located."

Many years later, Josef wrote to Knut's widow, Helene Ångström: "We built it narrow gauge with 125 pound steel rail and equipped it with locomotives and cars for $5,000 per mile. Their expert, Mr. Ilsley, said it was the cheapest railroad in the U.S. The State of Florida donated 134,000 acres for the railroad and private persons donated 66,000 acres."

Regarding the naming of St. Petersburg, Ivar Pearson relates: "In 1887, when construction was well underway and post offices were being established along the line, the question arose as to what name should be given the southern terminus of the Orange Belt. Mrs. Ella Ward, who had been appointed Post Mistress of the little settlement (a fishing village known as Wardsville), wanted it to have a name. Speaking to one of the more prominent people of the place, she was advised that the town should be named after one of the original four backers of the Road—Demens, Henschen, Sweetapple or Taylor. Mrs. Ward then went to Oakland where the headquarters of the Orange Belt were located, in order to confer with the four men about the matter. No one was there except Mr. Henschen, and she asked him what he thought."

Josef's answer is reported as follows: "They wanted me to name the town, and I didn't know what to call it. We had already named a town along the line after

Taylor—called it Taylorville (later renamed Groveland). We couldn't call the town Sweetapple very well—it would have been doomed from the start. And my name, Henschen, wouldn't be good, for no one could spell it. However, I knew that Demens wanted a town to be named St. Petersburg (after his home town in Russia). So I thought to myself, why not call the town down there on the Gulf St. Petersburg—it will never amount to much anyway, so its name won't make any difference."

"So I told Mrs. Ward to call it St. Petersburg. And St. Petersburg it became. I signed a petition, got four or five others to sign it, and we sent it to Washington where it was approved by the Post Office Department. That is the way St. Petersburg got its name."

Grismer wrote: "Hectic days were ahead for the Orange Belt. The railroad was in financial difficulties from the start. Shipments of rail did not arrive on scheduled time. The creditors began demanding their money and the supplies of the railroad's store began to run down."

"Thousands of acres of land had been donated to the railroad on the understanding that it would be completed by December 31, 1887. As this date neared, the officials worked frantically to get done in time. Demens spent much of his time in the North, trying to get financial assistance. Henschen, Taylor and Sweetapple, the company's treasurer, remained on the job, handling the thousand-and-one problems that arose daily."

"Then came the day when the creditors would wait no longer for their money. They went to the courts and had all the property of the railroad attached. The engines were locked to the tracks. Work was halted. The shock proved too much for Sweetapple, who suffered a stroke of apoplexy and died almost instantly. Some money was received shortly afterwards and the work proceeded again."

(Maybe this money came from Josef, as he later wrote he had invested a total of $40,000.)

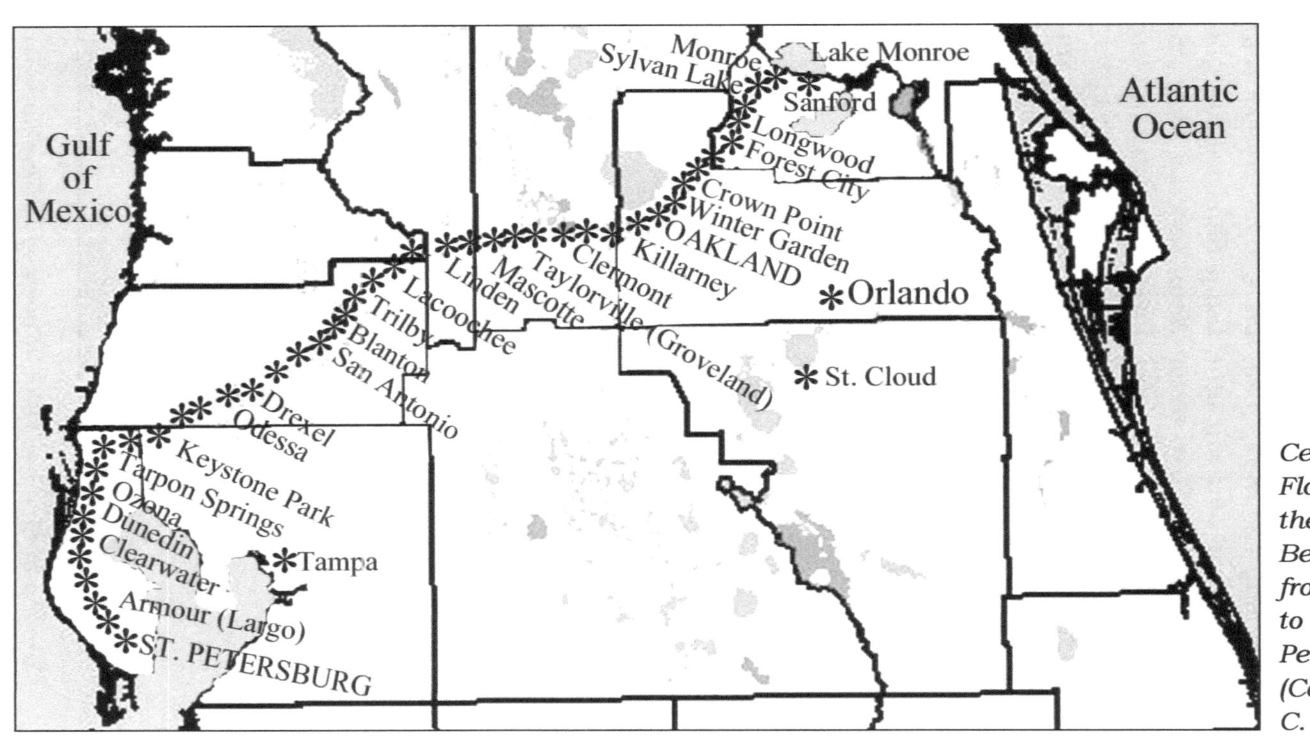

Central Florida and the Orange Belt Railway from Sanford to St. Petersburg (Courtesy of C. Best.)

The first child of Carolina and Josef had been born on May 25, 1886. It was a daughter and they called her Florence. A year later Carolina, who had a weak constitution to begin with and still had not fully recuperated from the first birth, was pregnant again.

On May 18, 1887, Josef wrote to his brother Salomon:

"Carolina and my little baby Florence are going to Sweden today. They leave New York on May 25; will be in England June 1, and three days later in Göteborg or Malmö. They will spend one or two months with Carolina's parents. In September she will have another baby. The old wound never healed. She now has large varicose veins which bother her when she moves. If she goes to her aunt Mathilda Wiström in Falun, she may visit you too, if you like. If so, could you please examine her chest and heart, because she has been spitting blood a few times and sometimes has pain.

Carolina in Sweden 1888. (Courtesy of Caroline Soka.)

108

If a change of climate is good for her, she could spend the winter in Sweden, to handle her health and study a little while I am busy with the railway. Maybe I will come home and pick her up in 1888."

Elsa (nicknamed Elsie), child number two, was born in Sweden in October 1887.

In January 1888, the railroad had reached Tarpon Springs on the Gulf Coast, and by the summer it had many stations, among them Dunedin, Clearwater, Largo and finally St. Petersburg. The end point was called Demens Landing. The trains started to roll, but the owners were deeply in debt.

The same year, in spite of his financial problems, Josef joined Carolina, Florence and Elsa in Sweden. They visited Knut, Helene and their first child, a son who had been born that year. Knut had become a prominent scientist who researched solar radiation, especially the infrared part of the solar spectrum. Josef and Knut did not have many mutual interests—the main thing they now had in common was parenting.

Orange Belt Railway depot in Clearwater, Florida (Courtesy of Florida State Archives.)

Josef of course spent time with his siblings in Stockholm and Upsala. My grandfather Folke was then seven years old and this was the first time he met Josef, Carolina and his little cousins. Josef brought shells and mussels from Florida for Folke, and this started Folke's shell collection which he kept up for decades.

In December 1888, Josef and his family returned to the U.S.

On February 19, 1889, Josef wrote to Salomon:

"Because of the Yellow Fever we don't have enough passengers traveling, immigration has stopped, and there isn't nearly as much freight as we had expected or what it would be under normal conditions. Also it has rained in an unprecedented way. In the four last months we had 48 inches of rain, when the norm is 50 or 60 for the whole year. And most of it in the summer. It has damaged the railway embankment. The harvests are destroyed by rain."

"I had an agreement with Demens that I would have work and payment until the railway will yield money to each of us, but Demens is in no hurry to fulfill this agreement. I had counted on working on the railroad now and earning money."

"Demens is acting like a Russian, angering everybody so that our traffic has sunk to a minimum. Times are hard. But I realize that with Demens we will never get any traffic. He has to go, or I will sell out if I can."

"I am going to the West coast for three weeks to try to get donations. Carolina will come out on Saturday and we will swim in the Mexican Gulf. The weather is marvelous."

"If only Carolina's health was better. It is up and down."

Much later, in a letter to Helene, Josef described the economic situation. "On July 1st, 1889, we had to pay $55,000 in interest on money we had borrowed. We were *forced to sell or go bankrupt. We had invested $140,000 ourselves, of which $40,000 was my own investment. We had to assume $26,250 for all the interest in the railroad and 200,000 acres of land. This was tough. I only got $8,850 for my $40,000."*

This was the first big blow for Josef. Several other financial catastrophes would befall him in the next few years.

For Josef and his partners, the railroad was a failure. But because of them—and perhaps especially because of Josef who had invested so much of his personal money and energy—the railroad was completed and St. Petersburg became a town. In the 1920s Josef said: "Where in the past there was an abandoned cotton field of 500 acres, there is now a city with 20,000 inhabitants, tourism and commerce."

"Had it not been for Henschen, the railroad project probably would have fallen through, and in all probability there would be no St. Petersburg today", Karl Grismer said.

Henry B. Plant bought the Orange Belt Railway in March 1895. One of its stations on the coast was Clearwater in Pinellas County. By 1896, Plant had built the Belleview Hotel in Belleair, right next to Clearwater. It opened on January 15, 1897. The building was the largest inhabited wooden structure in the world and was much admired. (It so happens that I live five minutes drive from this hotel, by the golf course that belongs to it.)

In May 1890 Josef and Carolina (who still spoke no English) had their third child, a girl named Elin. On November 9, Josef wrote to Salomon: "The children are a great source of joy. My family becomes more and more dear to me. Otherwise I am depressed, mostly because of business. I feel old, tired, although only forty-seven."

A child of Josef's neighbor had recently died, and everyone had seen the small coffin. Death had suddenly become a reality for Florence, now four years old, and Elsa, two and a half. The two girls were often talking about life, death, and the hereafter. Elsa took the matter calmly and explained that if she would die, they were not allowed to put her in a coffin. If they would try, Elsa would push up the lid and climb out. Florence, who was a particularly sensitive child, got big tears in her eyes when they discussed that Papa also could die, just like everyone else. "No, Papa cannot die!" Florence cried. "We will pray to God that Papa will not die!" She threw her arms around Josef's neck to keep him from disappearing. "But everybody has to die", Josef said. "Why?" Florence asked. "I will not allow them put Papa in a coffin and put him in the ground! If they do, I will dig it up and let Papa out." Josef asked Elsa: "Would you also be sad if I died?" "No", Elsa said. "But who would buy food for you?" Josef asked. "I would buy it myself. I would take all the money from the Post Office and buy candy."

Josef was very close to Salomon and Gerda and also to his other siblings and their families. He discussed them all in detail in his letters. Their father Lars had asked his children to love and care for each other, and they did.

(Following page)
A page from an 1890 letter from Josef to Salomon, on U.S. Post Office letterhead. Josef Henschen, Postmaster, is printed on the left side, and on the right side is the name of the assistant P.M. he had at that time—Signe, Wilhelm's daughter, then age twenty. She normally lived with her parents in Illinois, but was spending some time down in Florida. (Courtesy of Uppsala University Library.)

112

JOSEF HENSCHEN, Postmaster.

SIGNE E. HENSCHEN, Asst. P. M.

UNITED STATES POST OFFICE

OAKLAND, FLORIDA.

omkring 1890

ett barn sjukt (trol. genom dålig condense-
mjölk samt genom att göra födan för stark) miste
de det och läkarehjelp fagnade ej. Deras
lilla flicka ett vackert och frodigt barn fick
först maginflammation och tjöt ett och dag
sedan slogs bölder ut på flere ställen och sär-
skildt långs ryggraden så kom lugn men
stark feber och medvetslöshet och slutligen
daghenfoll och döden. Det gjorde stort intryck
på barnen och alltsedan har döden och
lifvet samt lifvet härefter varit ett favo-
ritthema som de stundom afhandlat
på ett för mycket realistiskt sätt. Elsa typer
ibland lugnt och förklarar att om hon dör så får
dom inte stoppa ner henne och kasta jord på
henne
för då kuiffar jag upp dödhet och kuipper ihjäl.
När Flores en dag sade åt henne att om hon
ej var snäll så finge hon ej komma in i
himmelen så sade hon "jo du, när jag dör och
får mina vingar och flyger opp så knuckj

113

Carolina had been very ill, but was somewhat better by 1891. Their Swedish servant girl, Anna, had been dismissed because she was insolent. Carolina now did all the household work herself, as well as caring for their three daughters. Josef was sorry he did not have better food for the children. "I would live in Orlando, where I can get fresh food, but I cannot leave the postmaster job" he wrote. (All Josef's children grew up to be strong and healthy, so he need not have worried.)

1891 marked the 20th anniversary of the arrival of Josef and many other Swedes in Sanford. On May 23 there was a big celebration at the Sanford House Hotel, attended by a large number of Swedes. Christine Best describes this in her book "The Swedish History of Seminole County". One of the speakers was Josef, who was quoted in The South Florida Journal: *"When the little village of New Upsala was started, the forest was yet in its virgin growth. Out of it was hewn material for many a rude hut and fence, the land cleared and broken and at such time that could be spared from work necessary to provide bread for wives and little ones."*

It so happened that Henry Sanford had passed away a couple of days earlier, and a tribute to him was included in the celebration.

Harald, the first and only son of Josef and Carolina, was born in October 1891. (In all the censuses the spelling is Harold, but Josef always used the Swedish form of the name, Harald, in his letters.)

In 1893, Knut had become a member of the Academy of Science in Sweden. Helene and Knut now had three sons, and in 1895 they would have their fourth and last child, a daughter. Although Josef was fourteen years older than Knut, they both married around the same time and had their children in the same years.

Swedish Midsummer party 1892, at Clay Springs, now called Wekiva Springs. Josef seated in the middle. (Courtesy of Sanford Museum.)

Letter 15 from Josef to Knut

(This is the first letter to Knut in ten years, and it is also the last letter to him.)

Killarney, Florida, April 15, 1894
(I live over the border to Lake County, but the post office is in Orange.)

Dear friend Knut!

It is now a year since I received your warmly welcomed letter with portraits of your little boys. You mustn't think, although it may seem so, that I am indifferent to old friends. I am not indifferent, especially not to precious friends from youth, like you. When you were a child, you used to cheer me up when I was low-spirited or had my melancholy days.

For quite some time now, my state of mind has been such that I have not been able to write letters. I do not want to burden my friends with my problems and adversities, and therefore I keep silent. In the past, I was able to write a cheerful letter even when I felt the opposite, but now I am too old to pretend. I write what I feel.

Still, I did start a letter to you when I received yours, because it really made me happy. My little daughter, Elin, who then was two or three years old, saw the portraits of the little boys, and knew my letter was for you. She then scribbled all over the letter and told me happily: "now I have whitten (written) to the little boys"! She was enchanted by the portraits. She is a pretty little girl, happy, cheerful, sensitive, but incorrigible when it comes to touching everything she sees. Nothing that she can see or reach is safe from her.

Anyhow, a year with its joys and sorrows has passed since then, and I certainly don't want to live it again. You were supposing that I was doing well, but I had financial problems, because I had lost $31,250 on the Orange Belt Railroad business—almost all the cash I owned. And with the political changes that had just occurred I was sure I would lose my job as a postmaster and that a Democrat would be substituted. And that wasn't all. When we sold our stock in the railroad I received between $5,000 and $6,000 worth of bank stocks. They were considered as good as gold and easy to make liquid in case of need. I gave up many opportunities of beneficial purchases, in order to have this cash at hand in case I would suddenly die, as I had no life insurance.

The bank's business went well, and the value of the stocks went to 120. My 50 shares were worth $60,000. But then the cashier got the idea of merging with another national bank which had existed during the good speculative times when values were inflated. It was the oldest in the county and had the largest number of customers and deposits. Against the warnings from me and others, the merger was done. The other bank was in terrible shape because of thefts and falsified books and because their president and one of their directors had lent $50,000 or $60,000 to themselves, with their own endorsement or guarantee. When the thefts were discovered, the cashier and directors still tried to continue, because it would only have affected the reserve funds. But when the worthless promissory notes were discovered, it was impossible to proceed. At the last moment, large amounts of money were withdrawn and bankruptcy is likely. The Comptroller of Currency in Washington has seized 100% of the remaining stock and money and taken legal action.

The bank is currently being reorganized. I have no cash, and only about 1300 acres of uncultivated land, plus the rent from a few houses. That is all I have to live on now. I will lose my stock and be glad if I can escape distraint or seizure of the 100% now imposed on the bank. Otherwise I could have rescued half of my stock.

This is how things stand now and it has been a financially difficult time. The rents are small and irregular. I only have $35 a month, and since last year $200 has already accumulated in outstanding debts. I have to pay $100 a year in taxes, land and properties, apart from repair on houses. I can't afford to buy fire insurance, and one house that cost me $100 and yielded $200 a year in rent, burned to the ground last autumn. I need to keep a horse and hire a man, and I actually don't know how I am going to survive. I am as poor now as when I was a new settler, but then I was accumulating property and was single. Now I have four children and a wife. If they were older, I would be even more distressed, as I am now unable to give them a good education, and this is my greatest worry.

However, we do not lack food, and we have a house and clothes. You don't need a lot of that in Florida and we are using up the old clothes we still have from earlier prosperous times.

As you see, one's luck can change in this world. And still, I am as happy now as I was, or happier, because then I had no children and now I have four, healthy and strong. What will become of them God alone knows. But I spend a lot of time with them.

I suppose you may be somewhat interested in the children of your old friend. I very much enjoyed hearing about your children, the little you wrote about them. My oldest daughter Florence, who was with me when I saw you in Stockholm, is spending this winter in Chicago with her maternal uncle *(Per Svensson)*. He works at the Pullman factory, producing luxury sleeping coaches. During the hard times in the North he was here for a visit, and invited Florence to stay with him.

We now live two and a half miles from Oakland, where the school is. This is too far to walk for small children. Florence couldn't go to school. Therefore I was glad to send her to Chicago, where these is a good school. When you saw her, she was a chubby little thing. But here, as the children grow older, they lose their appetite in the warm climate, and also sweat profusely as they run around. Florence is now tall and slender. She is the only one of the children who looks like her mother, and she seems to have a good head for learning. After only nine months in school—six in Oakland and three in Chicago, and no schooling at home, she writes long letters in English to me. There are spelling errors and childish expressions, but for those who only speak Swedish at home, and even for Americans born here, English orthography is difficult, more difficult than Swedish. The children learned English remarkably fast. We had a mulatto woman as a cook for five months in Oakland. From her, and by playing with some American children, my two oldest learned English in a few months.

Florence sometimes came to me, asking about words she didn't understand, but she never got any education at home. Sometimes I spent a few minutes helping her with her homework, but that brought her so much ahead of her class that she had to wait for them, so I stopped doing this. Our two small girls have their duties at home, setting the table and washing dishes. They don't do it regularly, but with a bit of encouragement, admonition and rewards, it works. They are very useful for their age.

And now they are coming home. On this Sunday afternoon they have been on the beach at Lake John. This is a lake which after a series of dry years sank to 10 or 12 feet, leaving a beach of several hundred feet. Then suddenly we had a tropical cyclone storm with 12 inches of rain, which filled the lake in a couple of days. I recall that in 1871 we had 24 inches of rain in a week—two cyclones closely following one another.

Now the children are rushing off the wagon, carrying oranges, sour wild ones and sweet cultivated ones. They picked them at a place where an old warrior from the civil war settled, cleared the land and planted oranges twelve or fourteen years ago. His heirs cannot agree on the inheritance, so now this orchard is on a lovely little cape in the lake, deserted, overgrown by bushes and wild vine.

My wife and I stayed home, and Anna Dahlström took the kids on the excursion. Anna is an Upsala girl we took in five and a half years ago, and who now has grown up to be a young lady in silk and lace, after she got spruced up a bit in Macon and Atlanta.

Now it is evening. The two youngest children want to sit on Papa's lap and want me to sing for them. Sometimes they want children's songs, sometimes religious hymns. Sometimes they want their own adventures described like in a ballad, in which the rhyme and metrical form is less important, as long as it is fast. Then they shout: mowe, mowe (more) and when they recognize themselves in the song they shout: "thas (that is) me Papa!" The cows Mollie and Rosa, and the steer and the horse also frequently figure in their imagination.

A beautiful moonlight is now beaming down and a cool breeze comes from the lake after a warm day. We live only 250 feet from the beach of Lake Apopka, the second-largest lake in Florida. It is about 12-15 miles wide. By the shore I have left a small piece of wilderness, a row of palms and magnolias. The latter are blooming now and their enormous flowers emanate an almost suffocating fragrance. Among the trees are also a few hickory, oak, ash and some other trees from a more northern climate. The water level in the lake sank 4 feet and left a hard, firm beach between 50 and 100 feet wide. On the northern and western sides are 28,000 acres of rich, arable swamp soil or moss soil, although not made of moss. I sometimes go down there at night, lie on the small dock and look at the moon and think about Sweden, or what I could have done with this lovely place if I hadn't lost my money.

But what I can do is to grow potatoes. It is less poetic than the moon, or my dreams, or palm trees and sweet magnolias. I have an acre of Irish potatoes, here called "Swedish". I hope to obtain 50 or 60 barrels, which are currently worth $500- $800 per barrel. They will be ready in a month.

Supper with the children is waiting. Oatmeal and milk or bread and cheese.

16 April. I see that I have given you no good news, only a bunch of fantasies mixed up with some practical things. Now I will try to write something more suitable for a scientist of physics and mathematics like you. On August 7 last year, the Democrats fired me from my job as the postmaster. The very same day I was shocked to hear that the bank had closed its doors. I had no idea they had been having trouble. The job robbed me of $600 per year. The bank closing decreased my income by $400 a year. In October the house in Oakland burnt down—a loss of $200 a year. My family was at that time on the West coast on vacation. I was in Oakland, ill—problems with my liver and digestion. With only $10 left, I joined my family on the West coast and lived on fish, sunshine and love. Large quantities of all those, but the diet didn't vary much. I wasn't getting better, so we returned to this place, two and a

half miles from Oakland, three quarters of a mile from Killarney. I now had $2.50 left. I did have good credit, but decided not to use it. I couldn't raise the rents, because everyone was lacking money, blaming the financial crisis. I got some food items from a merchant who rented the house that later burnt down, but his stocks were almost empty. It was a difficult time. I was ill the whole autumn, had no strength, was up one day, in bed the next. My wife was also, as always, sickly and sometimes bedridden.

In November I bought a cow with a sick calf, on credit. I cured the calf. In the beginning I only got enough milk for coffee or tea, but gradually I got more, and now I get a gallon a day. I hired workers for $1500 a month plus food, on the condition that $500 was paid in cash and the rest in future land purchase. Then I cleared half an acre of rich swamp soil, and am plowing it now with the horse.

We have a half acre vegetable garden and one acre of potatoes. Almost all the vegetables used in Sweden are cultivated here too, in the *winter*—like cabbage, cauliflower, kale, turnips, carrots, onions and radishes. We eat lots of these every day. We don't have beans, green peas and cucumbers, but only because we have not planted them. We do have tomatoes, a gift from the Gods for the liver. So far it is only an experimental garden. This autumn I will start working seriously and will plant every kind of vegetable. One harvest is ready before Christmas, and we plant another one in January and February, which will be ready in April, May and June. In July and August it is so warm that northern vegetables don't grow here. Possibly tomatoes may grow, if they are in the shade. In August, September and October we plant seeds for our autumn harvest. It will take about 10 years of hard work and privation to make up for the wealth I lost.

$38,250 doesn't grow on trees. I also have debts to pay but I obviously can't pay them at the moment. Even an old horse has to be bought on credit. I am hoping for better times and hope that I can sell a bit of land now and then. Even in a worst case, nobody can take away the 120 acres that I live on. The law here allows every head of family 160 acres, whatever the value of it is, and $1000 of property that will be exempt from all debts. Until now, nobody has tried to sue me. I hope to handle it and get a loan, although that is hard in these times. I owed the bank $700, apart from having lost my stocks.

But enough now about boring business, which can't interest you except to understand your old friend's conditions. The details are of course only for your own information. The rest of my property, including that which is in my wife's name, is worth about $20,000. But that doesn't help us, since it only gives us an income of about $300, and is hard to sell.

I want to tell you about our children who are living here with us: Elsa is six years old, has dark eyes, is dreamy, affectionate, emotional, unreasonable, stubborn, unselfish and practical, when she wants. Elin is almost four, dark eyes, blonde, slender, laughs, cries, plays, is mischievous, is both a child and a woman in everything she does. Then *the boy*, Harald, brown eyes, white-blond hair, solidly built like a Viking, weighs 41 pounds, two and a half years old, stubborn as a bulldog. "I don't want to! I don't want to!" he shouts so the house shakes, and it doesn't help to smack him. But a kind word always makes him mellow, and he is the most polite and friendly of all the children. However, his moods change quickly. I cannot bend him without crushing him, and I don't want to do that. He and all the kids are so fond of their mother and father that the smallest punishment almost overwhelms them. After a punishment they are twice a obliging. If any of us has to go out, there is no end to the tears and goodbyes, and then they speak incessantly about the absent parent.

I try to introduce some religious concepts, but sometimes they misunderstand them. "When I get my wings I will fly to heaven, and I will not let you in," one sister said to the other. "I will put the lid on, so that you can't get in." Little Elin doubts what she doesn't see. "They say God is in the room," she said one day at the dinner table, "but I don't believe it, cause I can't see him." "Oh yes Elin," Harald said, only two years old, "God is everywhere, everywhere!" making big gestures with his hands.

Harald has large head. I, not having a small head myself, can use his hat in an emergency. Like you did, when you were a child, he has a wide forehead. His head is so wide that he has two vertices. The back of the head which houses the "animal passions" is not well developed. It comes almost straight up from his neck. But judging from his demand for food and his obstinacy, he has plenty of passion. His intelligence seems fine and he conjugates verbs with great accuracy. Too bad that he sometimes stutters a bit. He had a cold and a fever last autumn, and a minor stroke. When he woke up he stuttered. He is so chubby and robust that a fever has a strong effect on him. Every time he has had a fever since then, he has stuttered. Then the stutter goes away. But when he is eager you can hear it. Hope it will vanish completely as he grows up. As the only son he is of course precious.

I recall how your mother and father looked at you when you were a child, and told you how your eyes were shining.

It may be hard to make a man of Harald out here, where nature is rich but civilization superficial. Passions run wilder here than in a country with an older civilization. If I can afford it, I will try to put the children in a school up north. The general school here is practical, like our life, but doesn't impart much knowledge. One thing is good though—they do apply what little they learn.

Regarding the young university student you asked me about, regarding his possible prospects here, I want to say this: here, more than education, you need a strong character to be successful, and you need a good amount of self-reliance. If he is not strong enough to withdraw from social life in Upsala and work on his studies, chances are that he would fail completely here. Hundreds or thousands of people who come from Europe meet disaster here, or become nothing but day workers. They lose their previous social class and are worse off here than if they had stayed at home. They don't have the strength to give up the needs and pleasures of the present, in order to rise above the average, create a future and become financially independent. In Florida we have no learning facilities that are higher than our junior high school at home. If engineers are needed, they are usually recruited from some known and reputable school in the North. I don't know of any field of activity for your friend. We have here a Mr. Lundgren, a graduate of medical studies, son of the late Reverend Lundgren in Sweden. He picks oranges in the winter, half-starves in the summer, and lives on credit. He is unable to give up wine, cigars and cigarettes. One of the poor boys I brought from Upsala, August Andersson, uneducated but strong of will and character, started out here by enjoying his freedom and indulging in pleasures. But he made a turn-around and worked so hard one winter that he was able to purchase a home and property. Now Andersson has become Lundgren's friend and protector. If Lundgren would become ill, he would be a burden for Andersson. I have tried to persuade Lundgren to return to Sweden. When a friend sent him money for travel to Chicago, Lundgren used the money for parties and temporary needs. So no, don't send us anyone with a weak character. They will fail miserably. Here, the laws of Darwin are more valid than anywhere—the weak will perish and the strong survive. If you can't take care of yourself, you will seldom find anyone who helps you or even gives you good advice. But hundreds will exploit your weakness and take advantage of you. This is an ugly trait in the American character. There is mercy for those who suffer accidents or unjust suffering, but not for those with a weak character.

I wanted to send you a photo of the children, but they have not yet been photographed.

This summer I will be fixing up my old field and planting an orange orchard. In five or ten years I should be prosperous again, if I live, and if I die I don't need an orchard.

Tell your little boys that my children loved their portraits and consider themselves their friends. One of the boys looks so much like you when you were a child.

My compliments and respectful regards to your wife and mother.

Your old friend Josef

18 April. *(First page missing. Seems to be a continuation of, or part of the last letter.)*

Page 2: The children cry when one of us is absent for a day or two, and are not happy without us. They are not, like the children of my second cousin (*Carl*) Holmer who lives here, happy when their father is gone and deceitful to him when they can. He has the respect, I have the love. I think Papa is their best playmate.

(This Holmer turned out to be the great-grandfather of Lynn Faulkner, who had inspired me to start researching the Henschen family.)

Today an American woman (not one of the best) and a group of British gentlemen and ladies came to my dock in a small homemade steamboat. The American woman asked my wife why she didn't join the party. My wife said: "I prefer to stay home with my children." The lady replied: "It doesn't pay off to sacrifice so much for ones children. They will seldom pay you back." That may be true for American children in general, but not for the ones who get a good upbringing, *which is uncommon in this area.* But I hope to create such a strong bond with my children, that when they grow up, they will want to stay close with us.

If I didn't have my family, I don't think I would be able to handle the misfortunes we have had. On the other hand, the misfortunes plague me doubly, for their sakes, for what I am not able to give them, for what they will be deprived of. But I am happier *with them* than I have been for years.

Nothing much to tell about general news. The Democrats are trying and discussing and planning to introduce free trade after thirty-five years of protective customs and tolls. The money and business world view them with suspicion. While waiting for new laws about customs, they don't know what to do or how much to buy, since they risk losses in a couple of months. The factories have either stopped, or move spasmodically to fill the needs of the moment. They don't keep stocks. Therefore, hundreds of thousands of factory workers are jobless or work part time with lower pay, to protect the factory owners from possible loss.

On top of this, Democrats in some parts of the country demand from their congressmen protection for *their* industry but are totally willing to have *free trade in other areas.*

Florida wants protection for oranges, sugar, raw tobacco and cigars. Louisiana wants protection for sugar. New Jersey and New York want it for various factory products. Ohio wants it for iron and wool, and so on. The result is a total split among the Democrats in the Eastern states where the factories are.

Democrats, with the help of congressmen from the sugar states, and from Ohio and Michigan, have completely changed the proposal of new customs rates which was accepted by the lower chamber, so that Democrats of the later type don't recognize it. We still hope, that with the help of the Republicans, the whole proposal can be thrown out, and thereby the Democrats' program, or that it will be further changed or delayed.

People in almost all the states are demonstrating their mistrust in the current Democratic government.

It is likely that the general election in the coming fall will strip the Democrats of their great majority, which they got by promising reforms and better times to the workers, two years ago. Unless some new combinations will arise, or some brilliant tactics from the Democrats, but this is unlikely. The Democrats, in their own media, already have headlines like: "The Party is in Great Danger!"

Well, it doesn't concern me, a potato farmer, but maybe I can become postmaster again and run the office in a rational way. The current postmaster will have to leave and grow cabbage. Those who are weak grow cabbage. The others handle the cash box. This is called Jacksonian Democrat Principles, and if they sometimes have to eat their own sour cabbage, there is no harm done.

Andrew Jackson, president of the U.S., established this principle when he heard from all the civil servants in the Whig party that "the spoils belong to the conquerors."

If free trade would be introduced here, all salaries and prices would sink to the same level as in Europe. Then, all public land would be sold and would no longer be a refuge for European workers. Even if this is good from a European or cosmopolitan viewpoint, the citizens of this country will never agree to it, when they truly understand the issues. The elections will prove this.

Not much to tell about Florida. In 1886 we had a late frost which did no more damage than freezing the orange harvest for that year, but it did create a general fear. The great immigration decreased and all property prices fell 50% and have never recovered since then. In actual fact there was great over-speculation, especially in wild, uncultivated land. I have always bought my properties cheaply, so that I could hardly have a loss on them, and have never sold anything without a good profit. But the problem now is that I can't sell anything because there are no buyers.

In actual fact, the immigration to Florida is now larger than in 1885 or before, but all the new railroads and new cities cause immigration to be distributed more evenly through the state. Land speculation is less. The large land companies and railways are forced to sell their land at reasonable prices, and individual landowners have to follow these prices. There are not many new orange orchards established now, but other new businesses of all kinds continue. If customs fees on sugar are introduced, or if the current premium on domestic cultivation is kept, large sugar plantations will be started in Florida. Rice as well. Here by Apopka 28,000 acres of swamp have been dried. Otto Fries is the engineer of it. It is excellent soil for sugar cane, rice and vegetables. The harvest of vegetables to be sold up north in the winter is splendid. Express trains run, packed with sugar cane, and in the spring packed with peaches, grapes and water melons. From one single station—Clermont on the Orange Belt Railway—60,000 bushels of tomatoes were shipped to the North last winter. Wagon after wagon of cabbage and early new potatoes and other vegetables were shipped in the spring.

We have two enemies—winter frost and spring drought. Many have had losses, especially in places which are not protected from frost by some larger lake, or because of their elevation. The very high sandy hills are almost frost-free. Low areas or those with clay under them are frosty. In a good year, the profit from an acre can be from $50 to $500 or even $800. Potatoes are now worth $2.50 per barrel, and new potatoes $6.50 - $8.00.

You must have artificial irrigation by pump, if you want to be safe from the spring drought. Some of my land is only 6 inches to 3 feet above the Apopka Lake level, so it needs no irrigation, but the higher sandy areas need it. An irrigation device for 10 acres costs from $500 to $1,000 depending on distance to water. Some devices cost $6,000 for a 15-acre orange orchard, but they don't need to be that expensive. We have plenty of millionaires in Florida who amuse themselves by making beautiful devices and outshining each other. My own plan is only to get a double pressure pump, either manual or for a horse or a mill.

I want to write something about our phosphate, but the subject is so large. We have fossils of mammoth, giant reptiles, manatees, turtles etc. Often you can still see the bone texture. You find these at the bottom of rivers, lakes and old river valleys, and in the form of hard rock phosphate which has no texture and contains twice as much phosphate acid as ordinary bones of animals. These probably come from lower sea animals that have been flushed up by the Gulf Stream. Recently a whole lake of several square miles, and also a canal that was being built, were found to have a bottom of hard phosphate, 80 or 90% phosphor acid lime. The company got $30,000 for it, with the agreement that the new owners would pay for the completion of the canal. Millions have been made from phosphate mines, but more through speculation than actual sales of phosphate. Now the price is down from $22 to $4.50 per ton. It no longer pays off to recover that which has less than 80% phosphor acid lime. Pebble phosphate at the bottom of rivers is usually 60%. South Carolina phosphate, until now the richest that had been discovered, was between 40 and 50% and once in a while a small amount of 60%.

How it can pay off to work on the poor apatite (*a type of phosphate*) in northern Sweden I cannot understand. It is remarkable how we here, while digging a well in the sandy hills, find excellent phosphate among the fossilized bones of sea animals. A Swede, Sjöblom, found a lot of those at 40 feet depth. Doctor Lönnberg made tests.

Let me know if he ever gave a lecture about Florida, in Sweden, and what his main topics were. Regarding his collections, he did not have suitable receptacles, nor enough alcohol or money to make any beautiful collections. He had to take the smallest and poorest specimens, as there was no space for others. He only had 40 liters of alcohol, when he would have needed at least 400 liters. He was a very decent man and I was sorry I couldn't do more for him, as I already had my own financial problems. Otherwise I would have loved to spend a few hundred dollars on expeditions with him.

I have a small snake now. It is brown or black on top and orange underneath, with black stripes going into the orange. On his neck there are two yellow patches. If you are interested, can you ask Lönnberg if he has this species? I have put it in alcohol. I also have a live king snake but don't think he needs that.

I have had some new adventures. I tried to help to take down a large branch from the hickory, which was damaged by the cyclone last summer. My right index finger got crushed to the bone. It got stuck between the ax and a sharp branch. This finger was already stiff from an earlier accident and had healed badly. But these are the adventures of being a settler and can't be helped.

The poor dog had to be dispatched, as he was useless in guarding chickens from fox and opossum. And one time the bull, who was getting hungry, stuck his broad head and sharp horns in through the kitchen door. The children armed themselves with wooden logs in case he wouldn't back down. We still don't have a fence around the house

Please give me some detailed news from Upsala, including news of my brothers and expected changes. I seldom write and seldom get letters from home.

Give my regards to your wife and children, from uncle Josef in Florida.

In the winter of 1894-95, the orange groves were destroyed by frost. This was another hard blow for Josef, but somehow he managed to survive.

Knut's world had its own dramatic developments. In the end of 1895, the German physicist W.K. Röntgen discovered a new a type of rays—X-rays—which received enormous attention all over the world. Olof Beckman, in his book Ångström, father and son *describes how investigation of the new rays started immediately at Upsala University. Knut, then an instructor there, repeated Röntgen's experiments with the rays. The dangers were not understood at that time, and Knut was exposed to heavy radiation.*

In 1896 Knut was a professor of physics at Upsala University. When the Nobel Prize was instituted in 1901, he became a member of the Nobel Committee of Physics.

In 1903, Knut visited the famous scientists Pierre and Marie Curie in Paris. According to Beckman, they gave Knut a sample of 100 mg radium bromide, which he brought back to Sweden. At the beginning of the 20th century, the damaging effects from radioactivity were still not realized. Knut carried the sample, which had a radiation of 2 billion becquerel (unit of radioactivity), in his waistcoat pocket. He suffered serious burns on the left side of his chest and left arm. This contributed to further deterioration of his already fragile health.

Josef's four oldest children Harald, Florence, Elsa and Elin, probably around 1897. (Courtesy of Joseph R. Henschen.)

Josef, Carolina and their horse, probably 1904. (Courtesy of Sanford Museum.)

Josef and Carolina by their house in Oakland. The younger man might be Carolina's brother Per Svensson. (Courtesy of Sanford Museum.)

On January 10, 1905, Carolina, only forty years old, died in childbirth of their sixth child who also died. Josef was left with five children, of whom the youngest, Augusta, was only two years old. Josef was sixty-two. Florence was nineteen, Elsa seventeen, Elin fifteen and Harald thirteen.

No letters from Josef to anyone about Carolina's or the baby's death have been found. Perhaps he sent cables to Sweden, but these were not saved. Six months later, in a July letter to Salomon, Josef mentioned Carolina's death in passing. He said Florence had moved out and was making her own living. Elsa was taking care of Augusta, nicknamed Gussie. Josef had a catarrh in his head which affected his hearing, and asked Salomon for medical advice. (He often described his ailments in detail to Salomon, and Salomon apparently wrote back with advice.)

Josef also mentioned that Carolina's brother Per from Chicago had visited the preceding fall, and he discussed his sister Maria, who was destitute and miserable as a result of bad marriages. Josef wanted to invite Maria to come and stay with him in Florida, but Elsa, who was now the housekeeper, would not allow it.

In a December 1905 letter to Salomon, there was a rare mention of Carolina. Josef said it was so sad that Carolina would pass away just now when his finances were finally starting to look a little better. "Carolina had a life of hard work, with very little free time or leisure."

Elsa also worked hard, and only now had her first short holiday since Carolina died.

Josef was sorry that his children had tough lives. "They have to work in their holidays if they want extra money" he said. "When we were young in Upsala we always had time and money for leisure. My children are deprived, and it makes me feel bad."

Later in the letter he added: "All the children are well behaved, happy and doing well, because they were treated well by their parents." (Apparently the children didn't feel deprived, although Josef worried about the lack of money.)

Little Gussie was still calling for her mommy, a year after Carolina's passing. Elsa, who was now eighteen, decided to be a substitute mother for Gussie and not leave home as long as Gussie was a child.

(Later, when Gussie grew up and had a daughter, the girl was named Elsa Caroline after her aunt and her grandmother. This is Caroline Soka, who told me in an email that she was very close to Elsa. As a child, she spent a great deal of time in the old Oakland house with its pull-down kerosene lamp chandeliers. Elsa never married. She devoted her life to taking care of Josef and Gussie, and died in 1954 at age sixty-six, when Caroline Soka was in her mid- twenties.)

Josef said to Salomon that he wanted to visit Sweden but could not. There was never any time off for a postmaster, except if he was ill. And if he lost the job he would be too poor to travel.

In 1905, Knut became the chairman of the Nobel Committee of Physics.

In 1909, his health deteriorated, and by the next year he was seriously ill. On March 4, 1910, Knut died, only fifty-three years old.

About sixty telegrams of condolence from all over the world arrived at Knut's home in the days after his death. Josef's was not among them. This is a mystery. Knut was a friend of Josef's family in Sweden, and they, Helene or the Fries family would have informed Josef. Yet there are no letters from Josef to anyone regarding Knut's death.

My opinion is that Josef was not good at confronting the deaths of people he loved, especially if they died young. I think he grieved terribly, but suppressed his grief and did not communicate his feelings. When Carolina died, it took six months before he even briefly mentioned it to anyone in Sweden. It took ten years before he was able to write about Knut, in a 1920 letter to Helene.

On January 7, 1911, Josef wrote to Esaias. He thanked Esaias for the Swedish- language literature they had received from him. Florence and Elsa could still read Swedish. Harald and Elin couldn't read it, but still spoke it, and Gussie didn't even speak it. They were not interested in Sweden at all, and even Josef's own interest in the old homeland was starting to wane. He no longer hoped or dreamed about making a fortune and spending his old age in Sweden.

Although the relationship with his children was very good, they didn't have many interests in common, and not a lot to talk about. They were not much company for Josef. He wished he could remarry, but it would have to be the right woman.

He said he still slept in the same bed where the children had been born and in which he would probably die.

Josef had shrunk from six feet to five-ten and a half. He often sat alone by the fire at night and thought about the transience of life.

Gussie was going to school on the velocipede that Harald gave her for Christmas. Elin had been teaching school for one year in Winter Park, where Rollins College was.

Harald had a fairly good monthly salary—$75—as a railroad clerk, and would soon have his own station. At the moment he worked in Ybor City (now part of Tampa). He belonged to the railroad telegraph operators union, which had a contract with the Atlantic Coast Railroad to get time off for holidays. Harald was tired of Ybor City because the inhabitants there were almost exclusively Italian, Greek, Spanish and Cuban. 13,000 cigar makers had been striking for a long time. There had been violence and murder, and the Americans had taken revenge. Two Italians, who had shot the accountant of a factory, were lynched. They were hanged the same evening as the murder. One of them didn't have time to take the pipe out of his mouth before he was tied up and hanged. The *corpse was photographed the next day, and the pipe was still in his mouth.*

Cigar makers used to spend from $50,000 to $60,000 every Saturday in town, and a number of merchants were now ruined. The leaders of the strike had been sued and would have gone to jail for threats and illegalities, if they hadn't fled. Only about 1,000 cigar makers had returned to work.

Harald wanted to be transferred "to a place where he could associate with white people"! Apparently he did not consider the Greeks and Cubans white. He was going to learn stenography. Josef would have preferred for Harald to save money and get a college education at Carnegie, Armour Polytechnical, Harvard or Yale.

Regarding their sister Maria, who was still destitute in Sweden, Wilhelm and Josef proposed that all the brothers make a fund for her. Each brother would contribute $100.

In 1907, Salomon's wife Gerda had died, fifty-five years old. Three years later Salomon married a young woman named Mary Piculell (1877-1965). She was Salomon's junior by thirty years and apparently not of the right social class. The new marriage was considered a scandal and Salomon's children refused to acknowledge or meet the new wife. Folke, in the autobiography he wrote at age seventy-five, did not mention Mary's existence.

April 29, 1911, Josef wrote to Salomon, saying he had had a catarrh in his head for fifteen years, and had arthritis and digestive problems. He asked Salomon for advice. He had also broken several ribs in a fall. And he hadn't had a holiday since 1888—twenty-three years earlier.

Josef went on to say: "My children, encouraged by your children's shameful behavior towards you and your new wife, threaten to move out if I remarry. They would take Gussie with them! But I would like a new wife." (Josef never remarried.)

June 17, 1911, there is another letter to Salomon.

Josef was no longer working as a postmaster. He was finally planning a trip to Europe, with Harald who was now nineteen years old. Josef wrote to Salomon that they would arrive in Stockholm August 15. A return ticket to Jacksonville cost $5, and to New York $35. Harald traveled free on the railroad. If they took the Red Star Line from Philadelphia, it would cost $45 per person. The boat would take eight days. If they took the White Star Line from New York to England it would only take five days. They would spend a week in London, a week in Paris, and a month in Sweden. There they would spend time with Salomon at his holiday retreat in the countryside, and with Folke at his summer house outside Stockholm. (Folke was now thirty years old and married to my grandmother Signe Thiel since 1909.) Harald, instead of going to the countryside, wanted to stay in Salomon's apartment in Stockholm. There he could meet young people and have a social life. Josef hoped to take his sister Maria out to the country for a few weeks, to cheer her up.

Harald had to be back in Florida on October 10, as superintendent of the railroad, otherwise he would lose his job which was to steer and control the movements of the trains.

Florence and Harald had volunteered to lend Josef money for the trip. Harald really wanted to go. Josef thought it might be the only chance Harald would ever get to make a trip like this, and he was right. Harald never returned to Europe.

Josef added: "You, Salomon, have been too liberal to your children—you continue to give them financial support in spite of their bad behavior. It is shameful that they are so prejudiced against Mary and don't want to see her, or even pretend to be civil or polite. They could at least keep up appearances and make some formal visits to greet her."

It seems like Josef and Harald had a good time in Europe and Sweden. Harald got to meet his Swedish

Harald as a young man. (Courtesy of Joseph R. Henschen.)

relatives for the first time. For Josef it was the last time he saw his siblings and their children.

By November 1911 Harald and Josef were both back in the U.S. From Florida Josef kept writing to Salomon until the end of his life.

In 1915 Florence had been married to Henry Bevis, M.D., for two years, and they had a baby boy. They lived in Arcadia, Florida. That year Elsa was twenty-seven and still living at home, as promised, because Gussie was only twelve. Elin was twenty-five, had left home but was not yet married. Harald, twenty-three, was also still single but lived at home. He had left his railroad job and was working as a farmer.

I have a letter from Josef to his daughter Elin, dated January 6, 1916.

"Dear little Elin,

Thanks for your short visit. As I am growing old I never know when I will see you all together again. I wish my circumstances were such that I could keep you at home. But that will hardly be before the grove which we are planting now will become bearing. Maybe I will never see that time, but remember that Papa sacrificed a good deal of his own pleasure and comfort to provide for you. All I now have is the $800 interest money I get, which in less than three years will probably be reduced to $600, as I may not get 10% again. However, I do it gladly if it can secure your comfort in coming years. I guess Harald can take care of himself, but you will be worn out by and by, and glad to have a home to go to. I *wish Elsie would learn some trade by which she could earn an independent living if needed, but she is fast getting to the age where she believes it would lower her dignity to work for a living. Gussie I guess will have to try the teacher's trade if she is not considered unfit for it. Her temper is so strong—she nearly went into hysterics when Elsie boxed her ears. Well, we will do our best and have to take things as they come."*

Josef went on to explain the history of the three silver spoons that Elin had received in the division of Josef's few heirlooms. The spoons came from Sweden and had belonged to Josef's father and grandfather.

"Now Elin, take good care of these spoons. If you ever marry and have children the dessert spoon will come in handy."

"Thursday January 7th. It rained last night but today the sky is clear blue and the sun shining. Pinky had written that he would come yesterday and Elsie was dressed up and ready for supper but she was disappointed, poor girl. If Elsie will ever marry it will be to somebody out of the ordinary. Pinky helps her wash the dishes and that has affected her heart. He sure will provide and make a living if there are any pickings to be had. He has been a sailor, a common laborer and a jack of all trades. If he succeeds as an R.M.C. (railway mail clerk) he will get $90 a month with a chance to work up to $120."

"Harald is fertilizing and harrowing the Milholland grove and will haul fertilizers until the evening. I will try to plant some trees."

The First World War had started in 1914. In April 1917, America joined the war against Germany, and by the next year more than 42,000 Floridians were in the armed forces. Florence's husband served in the U.S. Army Medical Corps. Three of Rudolf Henschen's (Josef's cousin) sons were drafted. For some reason Harald did not have to serve in the war. He was still a farmer and had just married a girl named Helen Iserman. Josef, although he didn't say so, must have been relieved that his only son was not risking his life. Over a thousand Floridians were killed in WWI.

Sweden did not enter the war, so Knut's sons were not risking their lives either.

Ten years after Knut's death, his widow Helene sent a letter to Josef.

Letter 1 from Josef to Helene

Oakland, May 7, 1920

Dear Helene,

Thank you so much for your letter with news about your children. (*Knut and Helene had three sons and a daughter.*) I am grateful that after nearly half a century in a foreign country, I still have friends in Sweden who remember me. Our bond is in the past, in the memory of *him* who left us too early, but who is remembered and honored by those who still live.

I don't work much anymore. I have left the maintenance of the orange plantations to Harald, who also cultivates vegetables and sends them to the north. Right now he is shipping new potatoes, cucumber and cabbage. Our lettuce harvest was destroyed by cold rain in January and February. We have had a wet and cold winter but hardly any frost, except on moss soil and lowlands.

Harald left a good position as Chief Clerk by the railway, because he didn't like the sedentary office work. He is skilled at accounting and telegraphy, and he can use a typewriter without looking at the keyboard. They have offered him the post back, whenever he wants. There he would earn as much as I earn from my whole small capital $13,000 with 8% a month—about $100 a month.

I have been working here for more than 49 years, but have lost $44,000 on building a 153-mile railroad, on three fires, and on unsecured loans to friends. This year my neighbors sold their oranges and vegetables for more than my whole capital. Harald wants me to invest the capital in planting new orange orchards, and enforce their growth with artificial chemical fertilizers, but I don't feel like risking my small capital. If he should fail, he has his abilities and knowledge to fall back on, but I would have nothing.

There is frost in Florida, we have had heavy ones that killed or damaged the orange harvest. The worst were 1835 and 1895, and two lesser ones in 1886 and 1917, but the trees grow back again in five-ten years.

My youngest daughter Gussie has completed school here, and there are exams and shows almost every night. Tonight, all the students will give a concert. My automobile stopped working and Harald, my mechanic, has pulled the machine apart. It is a large old-fashioned one with a 45-horsepower motor and room for seven-ten persons. A new one costs $3,000. I bought a used one for $600 and spent $100 in repairs but it still isn't any good. It uses too much gasoline which has gone up in price from 15 to 31 cents per gallon, and is expected to rise to 50 cents. Every cent gives one million to Rockefeller, the richest man in the world. He has donated $400 million to various causes for the public good. Carnegie has donated $350 million. Both started out as simple workers and were good, moral, religious men.

Harald borrowed $900 from me and bought a Ford auto for $500. He drives 3 miles to Oakland every night. His wife and baby are in Kansas, with her parents, awaiting the birth of number two. For leisure he plays ball games and tennis.

We four brothers (Wilhelm, myself, Esaias and Salomon) are all good boys. We don't drink, smoke, curse, don't play cards or gamble. We love women, but in a decent way. We and our sister Mia are 382 years combined. I can possibly live another ten years, but I am tired of living without activities, just reading and writing.

As soon as my orange orchards yield enough to pay for workers and fertilizing, I am planning to start a new one in a beautiful place by John's Lake. It will be shaded by large live oaks and palms and will have an excellent place to swim—a beach with white sand and porcelain clay, and highland with pine forest behind it.

But the orchards, which I have promised to my children, take all my income and part of my capital at the moment. Between November 14 and May 20, the children's orchards have cost me $420 for 700 grafted trees, $333.43 for labor, $142.50 in food for the horse, and $120 for manure. I have used $200 of my capital the last few years.

If I live I will clear land, plant a new orchard, build a house and live and die as a new settler, the way I started. But then I would have to remarry and hope for another bunch of kids. I am fond of children, especially handsome, lively boys like Knut, who one Sunday in 1863 sneaked into my lab. The next day, when the students were busy working in the lab, Knut hesitantly appeared again at the door. I waved to him and said: "Come in!" He came in and watched me boil and mix my stuff. I put him on a high chair so he could see better. After a while we introduced ourselves. I asked for his name and told him mine was Josef. After that he visited frequently. His sparkling eyes and beautiful, pale little face and its melancholy expression, due to infirmity, enchanted me more and more. We played in my room, and rested in the hammock between the apple trees. Since I didn't have a girlfriend, Knut was my dearest friend for many years.

Gussie just came back from the concert, 11:30 p.m. She has received new dresses for her graduation—two organdy, one voile, a bodice and slip of embroidered silk, two pairs of long silk stockings, and gray pointed (silly) shoes with high heels almost in the middle under her foot (cost $15). Helen, Harald's wife, gave Gussie a pale red silk embroidered coat and a large hat of transparent fabric... This is very different from her father, the immigrant who walked barefoot to save his shoes, and slept on the ground or in the woods, or under the wagon on journeys, to save a few dollars...

Affectionately, Josef

PS. Say hello to your children. It is past midnight here now. If we don't meet again on this earth, we will meet in the one above. The 5500 miles between us cannot separate friends. I am using a magnifier. I am somewhat nearsighted, write without glasses, sleep only four to six hours. I need to find a new life partner.
(Josef was seventy-six, but did not consider this an obstacle to finding a new wife.)

Josef and the Swedish community by the New Upsala Lutheran Church, around 1920. Josef is in the front row, far left. (Courtesy of Sanford Museum.)

Letter 2 from Josef to Helene

Oakland, December 8, 1920

Dear Helene,

Time flies and in two weeks I will be seventy-seven years old. I still have fairly good health, strength and mobility, and can walk several miles without getting tired. I have retired from active work with the orange plantations. My son Harald, twenty-eight years old, runs them with the help of hired labor. A Negro now earns $3 a day. Many of them come to work in their own automobiles.

I still live in my old house since thirty-three years. It needs new shingles on parts of the roof. The house has twelve rooms, of which five are filled with collections of old things. I don't destroy anything except money.

I have a cold that makes me tired, and I am starting to forget people's names and where my coat and hat are.

I am enclosing two portraits of Knut and his brother that I have made.

Like I told you earlier, I lost nearly all of my fortune, but my heart was not attached to property. Through twenty-five years of enterprise and strict economizing, I now have about $40,000 again, of which $15,000 is in stocks, $15,000 in orange groves and $10,000 in real estate. I don't get much joy from it. The more property, the more worries.

My three partners in the railroad are now all dead.

(In 1920, Josef was indeed the sole survivor among them. Sweetapple had died while the railroad was being built, Taylor shortly after it was finished, and Demens in 1919.)

Harald is a skilled railroad man, telegrapher, stenographer and typist, but he has a strong healthy body and prefers physical labor. His wife is from Kansas and they have two children. Florence, my oldest daughter, is married to a doctor, lives in Arcadia, has a six year old boy and expects another child. Elsa, now thirty-three, has been running my household for sixteen years, since my wife died. Elin is a High School teacher making $103 a month. She married a plumber, Gurganious. They leave home early in the mornings, bring their lunches with them, and return late in the evening.

I will send you some Spanish moss—they hang in long garlands from the trees here, on the sides where the humid wind comes. They are total air plants. Their botanical name is Tillandsia—Carl von Linne named them after his student Tillander, whom he sent to North America. We have three different kinds of it.

Best regards to the children from Knut's friend Josef

Letter 3 from Josef to Helene

Oakland, June 22, 1922

To Helene.

I have sent you a newspaper with stories about an American pilot, who had never before used a parachute. He jumped out at the height of 24,500 feet. A storm of 120 miles per hour blew him 30 miles away, and it took him 30 minutes to reach the ground. He almost died, because his oxygen tank was torn off and lost, but he survived. This is the highest known parachute jump in the world.

Our taxes after the war are enormous, to pay back the 23 billion dollars that were borrowed before the war. They range from 40% to 50% of ones income. One company paid 246 million dollars in tax one year. The army has been reduced from 4 million to 150,000, and in the navy, so many have been fired that half of the ships are out of use. Only a few airports are being kept.

The airport that was named after the Swedish pilot Carlström, (10 miles from Arcadia, where my son-in-law Dr. H.P. Bevis practiced during the war) has been closed down. Airplanes, that had cost $10,000 apiece, have been offered for $400 apiece. Many were sold to private individuals. I am happy to stay on the ground.

In May we had two weeks of heavy rain, which invigorated the vegetation. Then we had a couple of weeks of intense heat. Harald came home after ploughing in 102 degrees. I cannot handle that sort of temperature anymore, and mostly stay inside. I sleep well from 10:30 p.m. to 5:30 a.m. I put a log under my pillow to make it higher. When I wake up I feel rested and alert. All doors and windows are open at night and we only use thin sheets, no other covers.

My daughter Elsa, who is my housekeeper and "assistant postmaster," came home from an excursion with twenty-two other young people, to swim in the cool sulfur springs 15 miles from here. These boys and girls were from Orlando, our County Site with 10,000 inhabitants. They had supper, which they had brought themselves, then went to the motion picture theatre, and came home after midnight. They had rented an omnibus for $10 and bathing suits for 25 cents if they didn't have their own.

Best regards to the children
Josef Henschen

September 29, 1922, Josef got another grandchild. This was Joseph Raymond, Harald's son. The baby was born in Killarney, but the next year, 1923, Harald and his family moved to a house adjacent to Josef's and Elsa's in Oakland. Joseph R. remembers his grandfather as a kind old man. He bought large quantities of candy from Sears Roebuck, and doled it out regularly to his grandchildren. Joseph R. lived next door to his grandfather's house until

*1945 when he had finished his training as a dentist.
He then moved to St. Cloud, Florida, where he opened a
clinic.*

Letter 4 from Josef to Helene

Oakland, December 5, 1923

To the widow and family of my best friend Knut!

I hope you are all in good health and treasure the
memory of our beloved Friend *(Knut)* as dearly as I do.

Another year has gone by. I suppose it has been
a time of progress and success for your children, both
spiritually and materially. Hopefully, as time goes by, you
will keep having new reasons to rejoice in your children.

For myself, I am deeply grateful to Providence. I lost
almost all the wealth I had saved up with hard work
and privations. But during thirty-three years of small
speculations in land and property I have managed to
regain almost as much as I lost, and can calmly look
forward to my old age. I still live in the same house that
I built in 1887, when we built the 153-mile railroad to
St. Petersburg. I gave the town this name, to honor my
partner Demens.

*(Here follows a description of the railroad losses
which were quoted earlier in this book.)*

Josef continued:

I got $8,850 for my $40,000. I paid my own debt
of $2,000 and bought shares in a National Bank for
$6,000. Three years later the bank went bankrupt and
I *lost everything* except this house and 850 acres of
uncultivated land. I predicted it would take thirty years
to recover my losses, *if I lived*. I rented out my house for
$20 per month and that was what we had to live on. I
almost despaired, but started all over again. After the
freeze in 1895 we only had 65 cents per day to begin
with. I gave the postmaster job to my oldest daughters

and got a contract to run a 40-acre orchard, but made no money on it. Through small property speculations we paid for our food. I made 120-mile journeys with my two small ponies and bought wild sour orange trees for 10 cents each, planted them and later sold them for $1 apiece. I was not afraid of hard work and privation, which I now, at the age of eighty, could not endure.

But I have a 10-acre orchard which has started to bear fruit, and another 10 acres newly planted which will yield an income in three or four years. I have promised everything to the children. Right now I am making a new small orchard by a pretty lake where I have 22 acres. If I live until I am ninety, we will all have profitable orchards. I have this house and two small cottages that I rent out for $24, and I am building another nice small house in the Negro Town, where I already have two houses.

This summer I am planning to go to the mountains in North Carolina to buy a summer house and plant apples. I want to be active as long as I live.

Merry Christmas to all of you, from Knut's friend Josef Henschen

Letter 5 from Josef to Helene

Oakland, December 26, 1923

Dearest Friends—Knut's widow and children!

When last Saturday I turned eighty I thought about Knut and about you as well. The friendship with him, and the dear memories of it, are of the indelible, unforgettable kind. I still vividly recall that Sunday in 1863, when I was working in the chemical laboratory to check up on a chemical synthetic operation which needed daily control. The door was quietly opened and I saw a little boy with shining brown eyes. I asked him

Josef eighty years old. (Courtesy of Joseph R. Henschen.)

in a friendly manner to come in, and he did. I have always liked children, and was immediately enthralled by the boy's intelligent, reserved manner and beautiful face. He played in the lab for a while, and when he left

I said: "Come again." He came back the next day. The room was full of students then, and Knut was careful to not be in the way. I put him on a high stool so that he could see, without being in the way, and occasionally exchanged a few words with him. When I had completed my task, which he had followed keenly, he asked what I had been doing. This was difficult to explain to him. Soon my name became known to Knut's parents. Our friendship grew, and one day I took him to my house where he was welcomed by my siblings and by Sofia Sjöborg, who was a substitute for our mother who died in 1854.

Soon everyone knew that Knut was my special friend. He came and went as he pleased in our home. A lot of time was spent in my room in the attic. I received a standing invitation to his home as well, but seldom went unless there was some special gathering.

Although I learned early to associate with merchants and workers, I was shy with other people. After my mother died and my sister was sent away to the famous Fryxell School in Västerås, there was no social life in our home. I was especially shy with girls, a shyness which has lasted my whole life. As far as I know, Knut also didn't have any girlfriends, so we spent much time together. I liked boats, but Knut's parents did not allow him to come along on my sailing expeditions. "We have had another boy, and lost him to disease, and cannot take any risks with the only one we have," Mrs. Ångström said.

It is too dark to continue tonight, as you can see in my handwriting.

December 27. I had just completed the first page when my daughter Elsa, assistant postmaster, came home from the Post Office at 6:00 p.m. and brought your letter. I didn't read all of it at once, but saved it for today, when I could enjoy it in peace and quiet. I am happy that you and Knut's children consider me the most intimate friend he had outside of his family, and that you see me as a friend and member of your family although 5000 miles separate us. Any successes or adversities that happen to your children will always be of great interest to me. It makes me happy that they seem to be successful and have established themselves so well in life.

My memory of times, names and places that don't constantly relate to my current life and activities is starting to fail me, especially names. I will therefore ask you to write me, when you have time, a memorandum. Write the birthdays of your children, their professions, addresses, marriages, etc.

If it does not sadden you too much, please write about Knut's last scientific journey, the results of it, his activities at the university, and his illness and death. I actually know nothing about that and I am interested. He was and is one of my dearest memories.

(Around 1920 Helene did write a detailed and moving account of Knut's death, and the time just before and after. It doesn't seem like she sent it to Josef or anyone else, but it can be purchased through the Ångström web site.)

You may recall that in 1888 my wife and I and our oldest daughter Florence visited you and Knut in Sweden. You had a healthy little boy.

But after that our correspondence stopped. Our interests were so different and there were no mutual realities we could share with news and advice. He told me to not disperse my interests and activities. I wrote about local politics, railroad building and orange orchards. There were no more letters, but I sometimes heard about him from others.

Interruption—a man from Troy, New York State just came for a visit, with a lot of children who gave me no rest for one and a half hours. I was hoping to finish this letter before the mail train comes, but now it is 4:45 p.m. and the train will come any minute. I sometimes run the 1000 feet to the station, to give a letter to the mail clerk. But there is no great hurry with this one.

On Christmas Eve I had to receive two young men from North Carolina who brought complaints to me, in my capacity as a Justice of the Peace. Elsa said: "Don't receive them today on Christmas Eve." I said: "The law makes no exceptions, apart from Sundays, and in criminal cases not even then." One of the men, Mr. Sanders, said he had owed $1,200 to a general store in Winter Garden, 3 miles from here. Then he had returned to N.C. While he was absent from his Florida home, the merchant had broken down his door and taken all kinds of things that belonged to him, his mother and his sister. Some of the items the merchant had sold, some he still had in his possession. I said I could issue a Replevin order and retrieve everything, even from the people who had bought the things. Mr. Sanders said: "The merchant has sold his store and moved. We have visited him, but he refused to return the goods or pay for them."

"But why don't you go the Justice of the Peace in Winter Garden?" I asked.

"He was present when the door was broken and agreed with it. He told me to go to you. He would testify in the lawsuit."

I said; "I can arrest the Justice of the Peace as well."

"Johan knows and is scared. Several people who have bought things that belong to me are prepared to testify.

I said: "Make a list of the things that have been taken, and swear to the accuracy."

"We did."

"I suppose they thought you would never return."

"Exactly."

I said: "This is a complicated matter. I can get your things back and arrest the merchant, Thomson, for burglary and theft and send him to jail. But it is Christmas, and if you are able to reconcile, do it."

I wrote a sharp letter to Thomson, scaring him.

Then they left and I haven't seen them since.

Soon the room filled with grandchildren and relatives of my children. Christmas Eve we had my five children and five grandchildren here. Harald's brother-in-law, with his wife and four-year-old daughter was also here, in my large room 16 x 28 foot. I declined to act as Santa Claus. The kids, full of anticipation and curiosity, ran around and tried to look into adjacent rooms. Because of the legal business in the morning I hadn't yet finished making packages of candy for the children or write checks for the adults. I hadn't been to Orlando to buy Xmas gifts. So I packed dollar bills for the kids and checks for the women. The Christmas tree, a small bayberry tree, was full of candles and garlands of silver and gold paper. As soon as the children had received a trumpet each, the ear-deafening Christmas music started, just as in the old days. The tree was standing on a base we have used for thirty years in this house. There was joy, fun and laughter. The kids ran around, showing and trying their gifts. One rode on his tricycle, one shot with an air gun and all was cheerful.

One Christmas when Harald was a child, he was hiding in a galvanized wash-tub. When his mother lifted the lid he jumped up with big toy guns in both hands and yelled: *"Your money or your life!"* scaring all the small children, and making everyone laugh. Even though all the children are grown up now and married or working, they still talk about that particular Christmas. And this Christmas was just as cheerful. We were fifteen persons, and on New Years Eve we will all get together again. However, my daughter Elin and her husband have returned by automobile to Jacksonville, 125 miles from here.

The general use of automobiles has shrunk the distances and made visits to family and friends more possible. Railway travel is often too expensive, and the schedule inconvenient. I don't like to go by automobile at night, but the children are not afraid of crashes. You can trust yourself, but you never know what unskilled or careless drivers you may meet. Accidents are hard to predict. This year, 14,000 persons have been killed in automobile accidents, a large part of them at railway crossings. In the city of New York, there were 7,000 injuries and deaths from such accidents in *one week*! I would rather stay home.

Harald and his wife Helen invited Florence to the motion picture theatre (called movies here) in Orlando, 18 miles from here. They are expected back before midnight. It is not suitable to travel far on Saturday nights, because you can be delayed, and the Sabbath starts at midnight—no more amusement after that for Presbyterians like Harald and two of my daughters. Two were Methodists, but Elin left that church when they complained that she occasionally went dancing. I am still a stubborn Lutheran, which is an almost unknown church here. There is a Lutheran church around 9 miles from here, in Gotha, a German settlement. But I have, during the last fifty-two years, forgotten my German and am half deaf anyway from the catarrh in my head, and can't grasp the sermons. A Presbyterian minister asked me to come to his church, promising to speak loudly and clearly especially for me. After the sermon he asked me: "Well, could you hear me?" I said "yes, when you spoke with your normal voice I got some of it. But when you spoke extra loud, and turned to me, it was like thunder in my ears." We laughed. The other night there were performances in the church. My youngest daughter Gussie Mink, who got married on June 10th, was dressed as an angel in white. She didn't say anything, but had a candle in her hand and lit a half circle of candles. There was song and music and a forest of plants. It was all beautiful, and ended with candy for the Sunday school children.

As I told you earlier, I had many losses that left me only with my house and uncleared land which incurred taxes every year, without yielding any income. I had six people to feed and clothe. Hard work and prudent living has become a habit for me. Out of habit I keep doing business, until the natural laws will make it impossible, and will end my life. The great change in life is coming closer every year. Whenever I consider some new activity now, I think: "What's the point?" It is all over in a few years anyway. And what comes after that?

For about a year I have tried to follow the advice from my brother Salomon. I have tried to avoid everything that may drive blood to the brain. And it has been the most boring year I have ever had. In July last year I had a stroke which, even after I recovered, left me physically weakened. I made a plan to get away from the constant heat here in July and August and sometimes part of September, and go to the North Carolina Mountains. I wanted to buy an apple and peach plantation there, with a house and some cattle. But kidney and bladder infections prevented me from going there alone, especially since I am single and can't afford to hire a servant. Also, nowadays I don't like to be alone. All my children are married and out of the house, except Elsa who lives with me, keeps my household and works in the Post Office. So instead of going away, I decided to build a garage for four automobiles, with a large room above it which I will use for storage. It cost me $300 to build. I have also built extensions to one of the other small homes I own. They each have six rooms. Harald and his wife and three children live in one of the homes. I also built a veranda for $150 on my house in the Negro part of town. I intend to build two more houses in the Negro town, where I own eight small lots. I want to renovate a two story house there, and also build a house in Oakland. These projects should increase my income. If I succeed, perhaps I can visit you all once again, one summer. I would visit you and my two brothers and others, although their numbers get smaller every year.

Now it is 11:30 p.m. and Florence just came back from Orlando. I have lent $2,500 to her, and $7,500 to Pine Level Fruit Co. Harald has bought a productive 4-

acre orchard from me and 12 acres of land all together. He owes me $5,000 and has not paid the promised interest. Lending money to children and close relatives is risky and not good business. Now you know the details of my finances. I don't work myself anymore, but spend time with the workers every day. Next year I will be very busy as a builder.

Good night! It is now midnight.

Best regards to you and your children from your old friend Josef Henschen.

Christine Best found part of a newspaper article from 1927 in the Sanford Museum. It says that Josef Henschen, at age eighty-four, is in excellent health and resides in a comfortable home a block south of the present Atlantic Coast Line Railroad, which runs from Sanford to St. Petersburg. The article is partly illegible, but goes on to describe Josef as active and walking with the vigor of a young man. "He strides with firm and heavy step, indicating energy and fire."

A couple of years later he wasn't so healthy anymore. January 2, 1930, there was a letter to Salomon, where Josef described Christmas with all the family and his youngest granddaughter Caroline—Gussie's daughter—who was just over a year old. He told Salomon that he had fever every day, a broken knee and other ailments. It was so cold that his fingers trembled and it was hard to write. 56 degrees inside, 48 outside. They had an ice chest now, which was totally unnecessary. There were 50- to 70- foot trees in the garden which had all grown up since Josef built the house in 1887. He was reading the Tampa Morning Tribune *and the* Orlando Morning News, *and watching Harald's two boys (Joseph R. and Hal) playing outside. He still slept in the same bed that he shared with Carolina decades before.*

August 18, 1930, at the age of eighty-seven, Josef died. Christine found a partly illegible obituary with the following headline: "Pioneer Settler of Orange County Dies. Josef Henschen, for 60 years a resident of this section, died in Arcadia on Monday."

"He died Monday at the home of his daughter, Mrs. H.P. Bevis in Arcadia, where he had been ill for several months [...] one of the owners and builders of the old Orange Belt Railroad, now owned by the Atlantic Coast Line Railroad [...] extensive orange groves, which place is still called the Henschen Grove in that neighborhood [...] having been a Notary Public for the State at large, for over 40 years, he has rendered the Public faithful service, both in Witnessing Signatures and performing the Marriage Ceremonies. People having little or no money would always come to Mr. Henschen for help and he never turned anyone down, often putting off his own business to perform a free service for others. [...] We have lost a good and honorable neighbor."

For nearly six decades Josef had been a pillar of the Swedish community. He was clearly a good father and grandfather, and a loyal friend. His daughter Florence said: "Our home was always full of Swedes who came to him for advice and help and he always gave it, even to drawing up their legal papers."

On a larger scale, Josef contributed in many different ways to the economic development of central Florida. He was one of the brave players who took great risks and sometimes lost greatly.

Josef was a spiritual person who kept his faith in God through all misfortunes and losses. This is a quote from an undated letter from Josef to his children:

"Above all the enjoyments of this life, love is the greatest, because it is the reflection of God's love to us, and to the whole world. God's love expressed itself in the creation of the world and its beings, its inhabitants, and in all-wise laws by which it exists, develops and

progresses. If we let God's love take possession of us and utter itself in all our actions toward all his creatures, we become more like Him, the loving all-wise and all-powerful ruler of this and all worlds. We raise ourselves through this love, and by a life in harmony with His laws and rules, to be more like Him and be worthy to continue an everlasting life in his presence. This is what your Papa believes. May God help him to live accordingly."

Sources

Josef Henschen's letters to Knut and Helene Ångström, and Knut's letter to Helene. Swedish originals belong to the younger Knut Ångström, Stockholm. Transcripts in Swedish available on CD through his web site http://web.telia.com /~u32400585/

"Sanford - Korta underrättelser om svenska nybygget vid Sanford i staten Florida." by Wilhelm Henschen, published by Norden, 43 Chatham St, New York, 1875. Original copy located at Augustana College, Rock Island, Illinois. Translation into English by Rebecca Weiss 2005 can be found in the Sanford Museum.

"Sjöborg, Sofia Charlotte, Journey to Florida", translated by Wesley M Westerberg, from the Swedish Pioneer Historical Quarterly, Vol. XXVI, January 1975.

Letters from Josef Henschen to his father Lars and his brothers Salomon and Esaias. Letters from Esaias to Lars. These are originals, in Swedish, and can all be found in the Henschen Archives at Uppsala University Library, Sweden.

"The Swedish History of Seminole County" by Christine Kinlaw-Best, Teri Patterson and Charlie Carlson. Published by the Sanford Historical Society 2001.

Sanford Museum, Florida—The Henry S. Sanford papers and various documents. Letters from Wilhelm, Josef and Esaias Henschen to Henry S. Sanford, 1871-1872.

"Min långa väg till Salamanca" by Folke Henschen, Bonniers, Sweden 1957.

"Vägen till Rebella" by Helga Henschen, Prisma, Sweden 1981.

"Kvinna, konstnär, alltid Rebella" by Helga Henschen, Norstedts, Sweden 1996.

Joseph Raymond Henschen's (Josef's grandson) verbal memories.

Caroline Soka's (Josef's granddaughter) verbal memories.

"Josef Henschen, orange grower and railroad promoter in Florida" by Ivar F. Pearson, Swedish Pioneer Historical Quarterly, Vol. XIX July 1968.

"Henschen—the Last Survivor"—article by Karl H. Grismer in Tourist News, February 16, 1924

"Ångström, father and son" by Olof Beckman, published 1997 in Sweden by Acta Universitatis Upsaliensis.

Photos and Illustrations

Index